MY DOG IS A
GENIUS

MY DOG IS A
GENIUS

Understand and Improve
Your Dog's Intelligence

David Taylor, D.V.M.

BARRON'S

Dedication

For Christine, my wife.

First edition for the United States, its territories and dependencies, and Canada published in 2008 by Barron's Educational Series, Inc.

First published in Great Britain in 2008 under the title *My Dog is a Genius* by Hamlyn, a division of Octopus Publishing Group Ltd., 2-4 Heron Quays, London E14 4JP, Great Britain

All inquiries should be addressed to:
Barron's Educational Series, Inc.
250 Wireless Boulevard
Hauppauge, NY 11788
www. barronseduc.com

Library of Congress Control Number: 2007921334

ISBN-13: 978-0-7641-3858-4
ISBN-10: 0-7641-3858-8

Printed in China

9 8 7 6 5 4 3 2 1

Note

The advice in this book is provided as general information only. It is not necessarily specific to any individual case and is not a substitute for the guidance and advice provided by a licensed veterinarian consulted in any particular situation. Neither Barron's Educational Series, Inc., nor Octopus Publishing Group accept any liability or responsibility for any consequences resulting from the use of or reliance upon the information contained herein.

No dogs or puppies were harmed in the making of this book.

Contents

Introduction

The evolutionary journey from wolf to man's closest animal associate has taken many thousands of years. Dogs, quintessential pack animals, moved in with that other pack-living species, Homo sapiens, and developed a relationship of cooperation and mutual enjoyment. Today's dogs can fetch thousands of dollars on the show bench and are used to do things no human can, sniffing out drugs, landmines, human diseases, highly prized truffles, and even illegal mobile phones in prison.

Man's best friend

The domestication of the dog by man is a unique example of symbiosis between two species. Both essentially pack, family, and tribal animals, they developed together to their mutual advantage. To man, the dog was a versatile, conveniently sized, multipurpose employee-cum-companion. Easier to house than a horse or cow and, unlike these devout herbivores or the strictly carnivore cat, willing to share a similar omnivorous diet, dogs quickly adapted to life in the home.

But above all, man found the dog to be **clever** and **intelligent**, and the purpose of this book is to analyze what these two words really mean. Are dogs in fact highly intelligent? Are these dumb animals in reality the complete opposite of dumb? Do they even display a certain genius? This is an animal that can be far quicker thinking than man's closest relative, the chimpanzee; one that can solve problems as nimbly as a dolphin; and one that constantly reveals a great capacity for patience.

Ancient ancestry

It all began between 10,000 and 14,000 years ago, possibly even as far back as 35,000 years ago, when dogs as we know them first came on the scene in Eurasia. Their ancestors are now believed to have been the smaller southern strain of gray wolf (*Canis lupus pallipes*) that can still be found in India. During the period in question, the gray wolf lived throughout Europe, Asia, and North America.

Other possible dog ancestors include the woolly wolf of northern India and Tibet and the desert wolf of the Middle East. It is certain that all domestic dogs sprang from one or more of these sources and that they are not genetically connected with any other species. The most recent research on canine DNA proposes that all dogs derive from just a few wolves tamed in China around 13,000 years ago. Because of their intelligence, versatility, and socially cooperative nature, wild dogs spread quickly all over the world, with the exception of Antarctica.

Early domestication

It is probable that wild dogs were domesticated in different ways in different parts of the world—some while getting into the habit of scavenging for food around human habitations, others when early man hunted dogs for food and took litters of puppies back to the homestead for fattening up. They were probably the first animals to be domesticated by man, closely followed by the pigs and ducks that also came scavenging around man's refuse heaps.

Selective breeding

Human beings soon realized the potential of dogs. They could turn their paws to many tasks and, as time passed, man began selectively breeding animals for various purposes. Importantly, he selected individuals displaying certain infantile behavior patterns that were not lost as the young animal grew up—a crucial characteristic of the dog as a supreme associate and helpmate of humans.

Gradually, a range of dog types that were specialized in certain types of work came into existence, as guards, beasts of burden carrying or pulling loads, fighters on the battlefield, or hunters for food. Later, some were used in sport or purely to serve

as pleasing, hand-warming companions on the lap. As the centuries rolled by, the specialization of dogs mushroomed with the development of breeds to focus on certain aspects or types of hunting. Finally, man and beast arrived in the modern age where guide dogs, rescue dogs, and police dogs demonstrated their various astounding skills.

At one time, many scientists thought that the process of domestication had actually dulled the dog's natural intelligence, but fascinating recent studies, particularly in Hungary, have shown the reverse to be true.

Revealing relics

A 12,000-year-old grave in Israel contains a skeleton of a man with one hand cradling a puppy. It is impossible to tell whether the puppy was a wolf or a dog, but the loving relationship is self-evident. In Ancient Egypt, while cats were regarded as supreme among animals and worshipped as gods, dogs were also to be found both as domestic animals and as the symbols of the god Anubis. They were often mummified, and either buried with their owners or in their own coffins. At Abydos, part of the cemetery was reserved for dogs, near the graves of women, archers, and dwarfs. Dogs were worshipped by the Romans who made sacrifices to the god Procyon in the astronomical constellation of Canis Minor and also, like the Egyptians, to Anubis in Canis Major. Ten-thousand-year-old cave sediments in Czechoslovakia and from a slightly later Stone-Age period in Yorkshire contain fossilized dog bones, and small sculptures of dogs with curled tails dating from 6,500 B.C. have been discovered in Iraq.

Original breeds

Archeological studies reveal that by about the beginning of the Bronze Age, some 4,500 years ago, there were five different types of dog in existence: Mastiffs, wolflike dogs, Greyhounds, Pointer-type dogs, and sheepdogs. Mastiff-type dogs from Tibet were domesticated in the Stone Age, and later used in battle by the Babylonians, Assyrians, Persians, and Greeks. Wolflike dogs gave rise to the modern Spitz-type dogs such as the Elkhound, Siberian Husky, Keeshond, and Eskimo Dog. The Greyhound, valued as a skilled hunter by sight, is one of the oldest types, identified from drawings on Mesopamian pottery dating back 8,000 years. It shares common

SMART DOG TALE

Endal is a Labrador Retriever owned by Allen Parton, a partially paralyzed Gulf War veteran who is now confined to a wheelchair. When Allen wakes each morning, Endal removes the bed covers with his teeth and pushes his master's legs around so that he can get into the wheelchair. That done, the dog goes to collect the newspapers. If necessary, he will accompany Allen to the ATM to withdraw money—Endal takes the card and inserts it into the machine, then retrieves both card and cash. All Allen has to do is insert the PIN number. He will then put Allen's clothes in the washing machine, fetch knife, fork, and plate for breakfast and, later in the day when it gets dark, turn on the house lights. When his owner was unconscious after being knocked out of his wheelchair in a car park at a dog show, Endal maneuvered him into the recovery position, covered him with a blanket, and pushed a mobile phone toward his face.

ancestry with the Saluki, which originated in Syria at least 8,000 years ago. Pointers were probably developed from Greyhounds for hunting small game. Sheepdogs, employed to guard flocks from predators for thousands of years, seem to have originated in Europe. Recent studies of canine DNA seem to indicate that the breeds most closely related to the dog's wolflike ancestors are the Akita, Saluki, Chow, Afghan Hound, and Siberian Husky.

From those five basic dog types, thousands of breeds were developed both by natural and artificial selection at the hand of man. When Europeans first landed in North and South America in the 15th and 16th centuries, they found at least 20 distinct dog breeds; the Mexican Hairless, Eskimo Dog, and the Peruvian and Chilean wild dogs are among the few surviving natives. Other ancient breeds include the barkless Basenji of Africa and the Afghan Hound. Over the centuries many breeds disappeared and only about 400 remain today.

Top dog
From the beginning, the dog blended into human society in a way no other species of domestic animal has. The similarities in social structure between the wolf or dog pack and the human family, together with the dog's sharp brain and adaptability, were the keys to the development of this unique relationship. A dog really does regard itself as a family member, perhaps even as a sort of human being (or the reverse—that the family member is a kind of dog). Cats, tame and friendly as they may be, do not. The dog's owner is the *ex officio* leader of the pack.

Canine genius apart, we know that dogs are *good* for people, not least because of a recent finding that dog owners have lower blood pressure and cholesterol, and are almost nine percent more likely to be alive one year after a heart attack than those who do not own a dog.

Visits from dogs reduce anxiety, stress, and heart and lung pressure in heart failure patients, and residents in nursing homes tend to feel much less lonely after spending time alone with a dog. Apparently the "one on one" with a canine visitor encourages the resident to unburden his- or herself by telling the animal about his or her problems.

The **mind** of the dog

It is a surprising fact that dogs are born with their unusual ability to observe, imitate, and communicate with people. They learn to imitate human actions quickly and with enthusiasm—something even chimpanzees with their larger brains have great difficulty in doing. But then chimps have never been truly domesticated by man.

Until fairly recently, it was thought that domestication had stunted canine intelligence, but we now know that the dog's close association with man from the very beginning of the process of domestication has actually developed and enhanced its intelligence. By talking to, playing with, demonstrating for, and instructing the dog, man (the owner) has expanded its mental abilities to the point where, in some aspects, it surpasses those of the higher primates, such as chimpanzees.

This can, and should, be an ongoing process here and now for any pet lover, in the same way as we strive to nurture our children's mental capacity. Canine intelligence should be maintained and boosted by giving attention, using words, sharing games, setting problems, and, crucially, training. Keep talking to your dog, and keep it sharp!

Scientific evidence of **dogs' intelligence**

Dog owners in general are utterly convinced that their pets are highly intelligent animals. They can quote instances of their dogs apparently displaying lateral thinking, solving problems, saving human lives in a variety of ways, and showing evidence of prescience or even telepathy. So what do we mean by canine intelligence? Can it be measured? Research by Austrian scientists estimates a dog's intelligence to be no more than that of a 14-month-old child, but most dog owners would disagree.

Owners' influence

Research carried out over the past ten years by ethology (the study of behavior) scientists at Eotvos Lorand University in Hungary clearly demonstrates that dogs are smart because of their relationship with people. It was thought that wolves were brighter than dogs because they would unlock a gate after watching a human do it once, while dogs will not, even after watching the unlocking repeatedly. The Hungarian team suspected that the dogs might not be as obtuse as they appeared, but simply awaiting permission to open the gate, because to open it without permission would be a violation of their masters' rules. So they proceeded to test some 28 dogs of various breeds, ages, and degree of closeness to their owners to see if they could learn to obtain morsels of meat put on the other side of a fence by tugging on the handles of the dishes when the owners were present. The

result: dogs that had a close relationship with their owners failed to perform as well as those, such as stray dogs, that did not. When, however, the dogs' owners were instructed to give their pets verbal permission, they were just as adept at getting the meat.

Another experiment involved testing the dog's ability to pick up human visual cues. Food was hidden in one of several scent-proof containers. The dog had to choose one and only one after the owner indicated the correct choice by pointing, nodding, or staring at it (see page 93). The dogs picked the right container immediately. Chimpanzees given the same test, however, performed poorly.

An ability to imitate

The Hungarian scientists found that many, but not all, dogs are very good at imitating people, and will quickly learn to repeat the same movement that they have watched their owners, or even a stranger, perform, such as spinning around or lifting a limb. After observing how a human operated a ball-dispensing machine, several of the Hungarian dogs had no trouble in working it themselves.

Unlike wolves, dogs have developed a powerful innate ability to pay attention to people, to watch, communicate, and work with them. They love co-operating with and behaving like people. Wolves, even when raised from cubs by humans, do not display such skills.

Top 10 intelligent animals

According to Dr. Edward Wilson, a behavioral biologist, the ten most intelligent animals are:

1	Chimpanzees	7	Small whales, such as the Killer Whale
2	Gorillas		
3	Orangutans	8	Dolphins
4	Baboons	9	Elephants
5	Gibbons	10	Pigs
6	Monkeys		

A capacity for clever thinking

Studies by animal psychologists suggest that dogs, like some other species, can think in quite sophisticated ways. Put some food in a hole and cover the opening with a cloth, and monkeys, apes, dogs, cats, hamsters, and parrots will all go and retrieve it. Grasping the concept "food put in hole, so go to hole to get it" does not require the animal to carry in its brain a mental image of the hidden food. If, however, you put the food under a cup, slide the cup behind one of two screens, and surreptitiously remove the food before showing the empty cup to the animal, it must assume that the food has been deposited behind one of the screens when out of its sight. To reason like this and then successfully retrieve the food necessitates the animal maintaining an image of the food in its mind. Dogs, some monkeys, and apes can do it. Cats, hamsters, and parrots cannot.

How intelligent are dogs?

So what is it about the canine brain and thinking processes that enables this? How intelligent are dogs? Comparing intelligence between individuals of different species is extraordinarily difficult, if not impossible. Even within one species there are serious problems. Intelligence tests on humans of different races and cultural backgrounds have produced highly contentious results and, on occasion, accusations of blatant racism. Certainly it would seem to be self-evident that intelligence tests for people should be designed to take into account cultural and educational differences. Tests suitable for evaluating the IQ of a New York stockbroker are highly unlikely to work as fairly or accurately with a headhunting Dyak from Borneo. And both may well be equally intelligent.

Things get worse when one tries to compare different species. Dolphins are "very intelligent", but, although they do highly intelligent things in their watery world, how do you formulate a test to compare them with, say, a gorilla in Africa? Dolphins could not hope to perform well in banana plantations, and gorillas would fail miserably at chasing mullet in the depths of the ocean.

Comparative brain capacity

Some scientists have tried a more empirical approach to the question of comparative intelligence. This involves calculating the amount of brain tissue that is additional to what is needed to control the basic bodily functions—breathing, blood circulation, movement, and so on. This "excess brain capacity" is therefore available for the animal to gain more information via its senses about the world around it, and to go on from there to construct conceptual models of that world. In other words, to think, to imagine, and to be intelligent by gaining and processing pieces of intelligence.

In measuring intelligence in this way, it is of no value simply to obtain the total weight of the brain alone. Rather we need some idea of what a brain of a certain weight is busy controlling and what amount of brain may be left over and available for thought. This is done by comparing the weight of the brain to the length of the spinal cord (the latter controls all those aforementioned basic functions) to give a ratio, which should be bigger in more intelligent species. Humans give a ratio of 50:1, dogs a ratio on average of 5:1, and cats 4:1. Using this method, horses appear to be less intelligent than dogs and hedgehogs among the least intelligent mammals.

The dog's brain

Although the modern dog's brain is much bigger than that of its most ancient direct ancestors, it is still much smaller than man's. A human brain weighs about $\frac{1}{40}$ of total body weight; a dog's $\frac{1}{125}$. The part of the brain known as the frontal lobes is where "intelligence" resides, that is, where problem-solving ability, memory, judgement, initiation, and social and sexual behavior are determined. Man, dolphins, and great apes possess the biggest frontal lobes in the animal kingdom.

Average brain weights	
Adult human	2¾–3 lb (1.3–1.4 kg)
Sperm whale	17 lb (7.8 kg)
Killer whale	2¼ lb (5.6 kg1)
Elephant	11 lb (5 kg)
Bottlenose dolphin	3¼–3½ lb (1.5–1.6 kg)
Horse	1 lb (0.5 kg)
Chimpanzee	14 oz (0.42 kg)
Dog (Beagle)	3 oz (0.075 kg)
Cat	1 oz (0.03 kg)
Rabbit	¼ oz (0.01 kg)
Budgerigar	¹⁄₄₀₀ oz (0.0001 kg)

The canine brain has more frontal lobe capacity and more extensive smelling areas of the brain than cats, while the latter have greater development in the hearing areas. The frontal lobes of a dog begin to shrink before the rest of the brain with the onset of old age, normally somewhere between seven and eleven years of age, and it is then that the first signs of senile behavior changes may occur.

Other measures of comparative intelligence

This way of intelligence measuring has distinct limitations. Applied to humans, would it not follow that everybody of a certain height and build was more or less equally intelligent, and similarly with dogs of the same length? That surely cannot be the case. And can the idea of "excess brain capacity" satisfactorily explain why some animals, including humans, are better at problem solving—surely an indicator of intelligence—than others?

As for dolphins, a professor of neuroscience at the University of Witwatersrand in South Africa has recently postulated that the big brains of these warm-blooded animals are not built for complex information processing, but rather, with much of their bulk comprising "insulating" supporting cells as well as "thinking" nerve cells, are designed to

The dog's brain

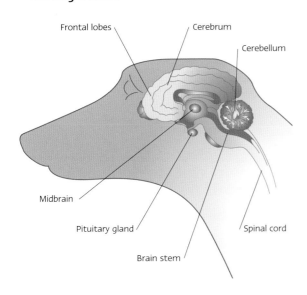

Frontal lobes

Cerebrum

Cerebellum

Midbrain

Pituitary gland

Brain stem

Spinal cord

Least intelligent breeds		Most intelligent breeds	
Need 80 or more repeats to understand new commands and obey a first command 25 percent of the time or less		Need less than 5 repeats to understand new commands and obey a first command 95 percent of the time or more	
Shih-Tzu	Borzoi	Border Collie	Shetland Sheepdog
Basset Hound	Chow Chow	Poodle	Labrador Retriever
Mastiff	Bulldog	German Shepherd Dog	Papillon
Beagle	Basenji	Golden Retriever	Rottweiler
Pekingese	Afghan Hound	Dobermann Pinscher	Australian Cattle Dog
Bloodhound			

withstand the low temperatures of their cold water world. Chilly brains, like chilly muscles, don't function as well as warm ones.

The very adaptability of the dog during the millennia of its evolution and development of association with man can, in itself, be held up as proof of the innate intelligence of *Canis familiaris*. A second method used by animal psychologists to compare the intelligence of species is called the ecological approach. It is easier to apply to wild animals than domestic ones. It defines intelligence as the ability to deal with sudden changes in the animal's

situation by using new patterns of behavior to deal with unfamiliar circumstances. It is the animal using its mind to conceptualize and extrapolate from one scenario to another—in other words to solve problems. And this is just what dogs have been doing ever since they long ago bumped into some hairy man wrapped in a deerskin and carrying a stone axe. But it is fiendishly difficult to quantify and compare such capabilities, whether across species or individuals. Nevertheless, some experienced dog trainers and animal psychologists have tried to assemble tables of comparative breed intelligence (see below).

Behavioral traits	Breed
High excitability, low trainability, medium aggression	Lhasa Apso, Pomeranian, Maltese Terrier, Cocker Spaniel, Beagle
Low excitability, low trainability, high aggression	Samoyed, Boxer, Dalmatian, Chow, Afghan Hound
Low excitability, high trainability, low aggression	Border Collie, Golden Retriever, Newfoundland, Keeshond, Hungarian Viszla
Very low excitability, very high trainability, very high aggression	German Shepherd Dog, Dobermann Pinscher, Rottweiler, Japanese Akita

Other breed league tables

Dog breeds can also be classified according to their behavioral characteristics following the work of Professor Ben Hart, an American veterinarian and animal behaviorist. Aspects of character such as excitability, trainability, and aggressive tendencies were considered for 56 of the most popular breeds by a panel of 96 experts. The results consist of breeds placed in groups of characteristics (see the chart, left, for examples).

Yet another list of 100 breeds compiled by canine pundits ranks them purely according to trainability. Top dog is the Border Collie, while the Afghan Hound languishes in the number 100 spot. Again,

this type of "league table" has its limitations, because it is hard to accept that all the individuals of each breed can be so precisely categorized, with, for example, the Bedlington Terrier ranked at 45, the Japanese Akita at 67, and the Chihuahua at 86.

According to this measure, that heroic breed, the Newfoundland, which, as well as saving Napoleon Bonaparte from drowning and leading one of the doomed *Titanic's* lifeboats to safety (see page 18), has displayed courage, initiative, and acumen on innumerable occasions, is rated no higher than 34. As for Afghan Hounds, breeders insist that they are bright, but simply don't obey human commands because of their independence of spirit.

Types of canine intelligence

Professor Stanley Coren, a neuropsychologist and professor of psychology at the University of British Columbia, Canada, has done extensive work on studies of canine intelligence and claims in his excellent book *The Intelligence of Dogs* to have identified three separate forms:

1 Adaptive intelligence

This is the ability to learn and solve problems. It enables an individual to adapt to its environment, even perhaps modify it, by quickly assembling information coming via the senses and processing it; calculating, if required, any necessary responsive action; and storing the solution to the problem in the memory bank.

2 Working or obedience intelligence

This is the ability and readiness to respond appropriately to various commands. In this case, a dog must be able to concentrate and possess a long attention span, without becoming distracted. It must also respond quickly when its handler communicates with it in some manner, and it should show mental flexibility in trying another approach if its first responses to a command are deemed lacking by not being rewarded.

3 Instinctive intelligence

This is the product of the dog's family tree and the long process of domestication comprising genetically determined abilities and behavioral predispositions that make the animal suitable to do a particular job—for example, Border Collies to herd sheep, spaniels to flush game birds, or terriers to work underground.

Breed differences

It would seem that a mixture of all three of the above types of intelligence is involved in any one individual dog. Clearly, however, a major difficulty in assessing dogs' intelligence is the fact that the various breeds, excluding the more recent "designer dogs" developed purely to fanciers' aesthetic tastes, were bred to be, and are, specialists in certain

SMART DOG TALE

There are innumerable examples of dogs performing outstanding heroic acts in order to help human beings in trouble and frequently to save lives. No other domesticated animal—cat, horse, cow, or camel—has demonstrated such close affinity and affection for people, and often with surprising prescience.

Rigel was a Newfoundland belonging to the first officer on board the *Titanic* when it collided with an iceberg in 1912. Plunging into the sea, Rigel guided one of the lifeboats toward the *Carpathia*, the first ship to reach the stricken vessel. Suddenly, the lifeboat began to drift perilously under the *Carpathia's* bows, its huddled cargo of survivors too weak and shocked to shout a warning. The dog, swimming ahead, saw the danger and began barking repeatedly to attract the attention of the ship's bridge. Its captain heard the barking, went to the starboard bow, spotted the lifeboat and immediately ordered "Full Stop All Engines." Everyone in the boat, as well as Rigel, who by now had been paddling for three hours in the ice-cold water, was saved.

ways. How then to set up intelligence tests that are fair to all?

Sight hounds, such as Greyhounds and Salukis, would obviously outperform scent hounds in tests involving visual clues—and vice versa. Similarly, the Beagle, a good hunter, displays what is undoubtedly "intelligence" when working out in the field that would not be appropriate in, say, a Border Collie or Australian Cattle Dog. The Beagle concentrates intently on picking up and then following a scent trail to its source. It will ignore all distractions other than the commands of its handler.

By contrast, a Border Collie working a flock of sheep must be able to juggle multiple incoming perceptions simultaneously, including distractions. It must keep the sheep moving in the right direction as a fairly compact mass, not too fast and not too slow. It must keep an eye open for stragglers, dawdlers, or fugitives, and it must scan the area around the flock for any sign of danger or difficulty, all the while with an ear cocked and the occasional quick glance, alert to respond to any signal from the shepherd.

Border Collies may be highly intelligent, but a potential downside of their sharp-wittedness is their ability to learn quickly things that their owner would rather they did not know and to get into trouble easily when boredom sets in.

Canine hybrids versus pure breeds

But what about the mongrel? All of us have met a highly intelligent mongrel mutt at some time or another. After all, the chances are that they benefit from possessing so-called hybrid vigor—the increased strength of different characteristics in hybrids through a combination of the "virtues" of its parents. One study suggests that hybrid vigor may be associated with increased intelligence in humans. Children of Japanese–Caucasian unions scored higher in a number of IQ tests than those from ethnic families, despite having virtually identical parental educational and occupational backgrounds. Some scientists believe that canine hybrids may have similar intelligence advantages.

How do you compare the home rescued mutt to the Borzoi or Bedlington? Impossible. Although most of us will allow that Border Collies are among the most intelligent, if not *the* most intelligent, of breeds, tables that rank breeds by their intelligence are contentious. There are plenty of exceptions to prove the rule. In over 50 years as a veterinarian, I have had dealings with some undeniably intelligent Afghan Hounds, Basset Hounds, and Shih-Tzus.

SMART DOG TALE

When I was a young veterinarian, one of my farmer clients had a Border Collie named Fly, who spent most of his days outdoors in the fields keeping an eye on the herd of cattle. This highly intelligent dog knew the normal behavior of cows implicitly and he was very quick to spot anything slightly odd about their demeanor. The moment he saw a cow not lying comfortably at rest, but down with spastically extended limbs, or a cow on new grass in spring began to wobble as it walked, a sign of "staggers" or hypomagnesaemia, he would dash to the farmhouse to raise the alarm. From time to time our clinic would receive a phone call from the farmer saying something along the lines of "Can you send a veterinarian right away? Fly's just found us a heifer having difficulty first time calving!" When I or one of my colleagues arrived at the farm, Fly would, of course, accompany us to the stricken animal and watch closely as we got to work.

The canine **character**

Dogs are complex characters with ways of thinking that are different from those of, say, cats or horses, and which in many respects resemble human ones; not surprising when for millennia they have watched, copied, remembered, and learned from our ways of behaving. As with children, their intellect is developed through social contacts very early in life, and each dog has its own, personal mental characteristics. Some of the most interesting canine personalities are to be found among mongrels. Inheriting genes from a broader pool than pedigrees, their characters are a complex blend, tending to display the strengths of each dog breed in their make-up, while at the same time diminishing the sometimes undesirable traits of many pure breeds.

Canine reasoning

Intellect is the capacity for understanding, thinking, and reasoning as distinct from feeling or wishing. Dogs demonstrate intellectual powers in many different, often amazing, ways, including by using logical deduction. Our canine pet, as Shakespeare writes in *Hamlet*, would appear to be "a beast that wants discourse of reason."

An example of canine reasoning is the German Shepherd Dog that loved to have sticks thrown to retrieve. On one occasion its owner threw a small branch over the garden fence, which was built of vertical wooden planks. A single plank was missing, providing an aperture through which the dog dashed into the field beyond. Seizing the branch in its jaws, it turned and began to trot back toward the garden. While doing so, it quickly appreciated that, with the branch held horizontally between its teeth, it would not on this occasion be able to run straight through the gap in the fence. So, still trotting, it turned its head to one side through 90 degrees. Dog and branch, the latter now held vertically, slipped through into the garden with ease. In similar circumstances, a cat carrying, say, a plump trophy rabbit it was bringing home as a present for its owner would butt away uncomprehendingly at a too-small cat flap.

Canine prejudice...?

Dogs can be prejudiced. They may show dislike or even aggression toward people of certain appearances. One dog might, for example, apparently detest men with beards, and for another, the sight of people carrying sticks sets his hackles rising. Some could almost be termed canine racists because of the way they behave toward certain ethnic groups. Canine prejudice is not, however, inherent in the animal.

The cause of such aberrant behavior might in certain cases lie in the memory of bad experiences in the past—being maltreated in some way by a bearded owner or beaten by a man with a stick. However, the society in which dogs live, its nature and culture, may also be responsible. If an owner displays antipathy toward particular individuals, this can easily be picked up by the dog.

...or rational behavior?

The classic dog versus postman scenario does not fall into the category of pets with irrational prejudice. Here, the dog is behaving rationally as a member of the family pack on the pack's territory. Unknown human or canine individuals are viewed initially with suspicion as being from outside the pack. The dog's owner is regarded as leader of the pack. If a stranger (human or dog) is accepted without aggression by the pack leader, he, she, or it will normally be accepted by the dog. In the absence of the pack leader, the dog, be it but a small, normally unassuming bitch, understandably steps in and takes over the role. Look at it from the dog's point of view. Up the path walks the postman. The leader of the pack does not come out to greet him. The dog warns the postman off by barking. Guess

what, the postman turns tail after doing some fumbling for a few seconds at the door, but failing to enter. The dog is triumphant. He has driven off this stranger who is clearly a rank coward. It only took a bark or two and the man was off! Each day, dog and intruder go through the same motions. The dog recognizes sooner or later that a post office uniform is the mark of a coward who can be chased and who can be expected to retreat literally post haste.

Social conditioning

The first few weeks of a dog's life are vitally important in conditioning it to the world around it. For example, if it lives in a society where bearded men are seldom seen, it may come as a shock to the dog when it encounters such a person later in life, particularly if the owner does not take immediate steps to handle the meeting with understanding and sensitivity. Sadly, dogs have sometimes been encouraged and trained to react aggressively toward human beings of a particular race. In apartheid South Africa, attack dogs were specially bred to target black people, and the extremist Herstigte Nasionale Party advertised them for sale as "racist watchdogs."

Irrational fears

Like their owners, dogs can suffer from anxiety, fears, and phobias (unreasonable fears), and, again, like those afflictions in human beings, they can be of many and various kinds, which can be classified into five main groups:

1 Fear of people
2 Fear of places, including fear of water
3 Fear of animals
4 Fear of noises
5 Separation anxiety

Personality test case

I tried out Gosling's personality test on Jumbo, a Rhodesian Ridgeback, whose owner considers him to be energetic, affectionate, calm, but a bit stupid. I asked a colleague of mine, who had never previously seen the dog, to give his opinion of Jumbo's personality using the four criteria. I did not tell him what the owner thought of the dog's personality. I watched as Jumbo was encouraged to play by the stranger, which he did with great gusto, chasing and retrieving sticks for 20 minutes. The dog was clearly affectionate, nuzzling and licking my colleague at every opportunity. We then brought on a Labrador Retriever that Jumbo had never met before, and Jumbo's owner was then instructed to walk off with the Labrador, at which Jumbo appeared totally unconcerned. The final test, asking the dog to find a biscuit hidden under a cup, was too much for him—he just could not figure it out. My colleague was then asked to sum up Jumbo's personality. "Energetic, affectionate, calm, but I'm afraid, not very bright" was the reply.

Effective treatments

In most cases, the key to eliminating the fearful state is training, and these training methods are explored later in the book (see pages 98-101). In a small number of cases, medication can be useful. For example, the hormone melatonin, used to combat jet lag and sleep disturbance in humans, was recently discovered to be effective in the treatment of noise-phobic dogs. In some excessively anxious dogs, anxiolytic (anxiety-relieving) medication or alternative medicine, in the form of flower essences containing extracts of such plants as red chestnut and mimulus, can be employed. It has been shown that, as for their owners, classical music by such masters as Mozart, Haydn, and Bach has a definite calming effect on dogs that hate being left alone.

Personality characteristics

Dogs have personalities and their characters, even within the same breed, vary enormously. Professor Sam Gosling of the University of Texas has developed a way of assessing the canine character based on methods originally applied to human beings. First, he asked the dog's owner to rate the dog on four personality characteristics:

1 Energetic-slothful
2 Affectionate-aggressive
3 Anxious-calm
4 Intelligent-stupid

He then asked total strangers to rate the animal according to the same characteristics. They noted the dog's behavior when tested for the four trait couples, for instance, anxious-calm was assessed by noting the dog's reaction when the owner walked away with another dog and intelligent-stupid was judged by the animal's ability to retrieve a treat hidden under a cup (see page 95). It was found that the test results correlated with what the owners said about their pets. Gosling's tests have gone a long way in changing the opinions of many members of the scientific community, who for long had argued that dogs do not have personalities.

Canine **emotional intelligence**

Do animals possess emotions? Can they experience love, hatred, a sense of loss, and grief? Do they even perhaps have souls? Throughout history these questions have been fiercely debated. The great philosopher Descartes considered animals to be but "mere machines." But read on and I suspect you, like me, will come to a different conclusion.

Humanlike emotions

There is no doubt that grief is an emotion that dogs can express. Take the famous example of Greyfriars Bobby, a Skye Terrier, who, after his master's death, followed the coffin to the churchyard and attended the ceremony, defying all efforts to shoo him away. The little dog spent the following 14 years living around the churchyard apparently grieving for his lost friend and master. A similar case was that of Old Shep, who maintained a five-year vigil at the railway station in Fort Benton, Montana, after seeing the coffin of his master loaded onto a train.

In Tokyo, Japan, each year on April 8 dog lovers assemble at the Shibuya underground station to pay homage to Hachiko, a Japanese Akita (one of the three breeds native to Japan) and another remarkably faithful canine. Hachiko belonged to a Tokyo university don, Professor Ueno. Each day the dog would walk to the station to welcome his master as he came back from work. After the professor died in 1925, Hachiko continued to meet the train every single day until he himself died in 1934.

Most of us would conclude that Greyfriars Bobby loved his master and Hachiko loved Professor Ueno. But are dogs capable of "loving" in the same way we humans are? Or are they simply skilled at using us to get what they want because they have learned that the "cute factor" brings attention and treats?

Scientists, philosophers, and theologians hold conflicting opinions, but among scientists at least there is an increasing tendency to accept that dogs have humanlike feelings and that the subject deserves more study.

We know that dogs, like humans and other animals, possess a "pleasure center" in their brains that is stimulated by the chemical dopamine. When dopamine is released in the "pleasure center," a feeling of happiness is generated. Love is a powerful factor in the life of dogs, whether as pack or family (human pack) animals.

Dr. Susan Eirich, a biologist and psychologist, says: "Strong emotion underpins social behavior and connection," and Leslie Burgard, a certified dog trainer at State College, Pennsylvania, agrees. "Their loyalty is unconditional—much like that between parent and child. The love and the loyalty that drives that emotion is instinctual...I think dogs have a 'love' or connection with their humans that is free of preconceived perceptions."

The canine soul?

A survey carried out by Dr. Bruce Fogle, a well-known veterinarian, found that one out of five veterinarians in Britain believes that a dog has a soul and an afterlife, and that *all* Japanese veterinarians surveyed (living, of course, in a Buddhist and Shintoist culture) believe the same.

Humanitarian behavior

Dogs are different from all other domestic animals in that they often possess close affinity with human beings, as can cats, horses, and parrots, but they, far more than other species, are capable of what one might term "humanitarian" behavior. Certainly a cat or a horse has, on occasions, saved a human life, but dogs have done so repeatedly, in many different ways and sometimes with heroic self-sacrifice. This can be viewed as another aspect of canine genius.

SMART DOG TALE

Dorado, a four-year-old Labrador Retriever, found himself caught up in the horrific events of 9/11 in New York. He was the guide dog of blind computer technician Omar Eduardo Rivera, who was working on the 71st floor of the World Trade Center's north tower when the hijacked aircraft struck the building above him. Here is how Mr Rivera describes what happened next:

"I stood up and I could hear how pieces of glass were flying around and falling. I could feel the smoke filling up my lungs and the heat was unbearable. Not having any sight I knew I wouldn't be able to run down the stairs and through all the obstacles like other people. I was resigned to dying and decided to free Dorado to give him a chance of escape...so I unclipped his lead, ruffled his head, gave him a nudge, and ordered Dorado to go."

At that moment, Dorado was swept away by the panicking crush of people fleeing down the stairs and Mr Rivera found himself alone amid the chaos for several minutes. But then the unexpected happened. He found himself nudged at knee height in a familiar fuzzy-muzzled way. Dorado was back for his master. The dog proceeded to guide Mr. Rivera down 70 flights of stairs, the stairwell packed with shoving, pushing, terrified folk. It took more than an hour, with Dorado nudging his friend down step by step, for the pair to reach ground level and safety. Not long after they did so, the tower collapsed. Dorado most certainly lived up to his name, which means, in English, "covered in gold."

The dog's **brain** and **glands**

The way a dog thinks is influenced by a range of interlocking factors—its senses, the situation it finds itself in, memory, instinct, its age, the state of health of its nervous system. and its endocrine glands. These organs produce chemicals (hormones), some of which can affect thinking. Some of the most active glands are the sex glands. In the male, the hormone testosterone exerts its effects nonstop after puberty, while in females, estrogen makes its presence felt on a cyclical, roughly twice-yearly, basis.

The link between stress and sex

The mind of the dog is, like the minds of human beings and other creatures, influenced by sex. They may not be "turned on" by erotic pictures, and they are not interested in, or capable of, learning from and copying films of other members of their species mating, as is the case with higher primates such as chimpanzees. They do not spontaneously think about or reflect upon sexual matters, although their dreams may well contain recollections of sexual experiences in the past. However, visual, olfactory, aural, and perhaps other types of stimuli certainly influence the sexual performance of dogs, and in order for males in particular to know what to do when setting about breeding, it is vital that they have plenty of opportunity to socialize with their own kind when young.

Hormones and the canine brain

With dogs, sex lies primarily in the brain and secondarily in the hormones. Part of the brain, the hypothalamus, and the nearby pituitary gland (the master gland of the body) are in control of the other hormone-secreting glands of the body. The latter return the compliment by influencing the canine mind. In the male dog, the treatment he receives from his relatives and other dogs in early life and from human beings later on, in terms of the range and nature of his experiences, produces stress within the animal, and this stress is registered in the brain. Responding, the brain instructs the pituitary gland, lying beneath it, to send out hormonal commands to other glands, such as the adrenals, ovaries, and testes.

Under stress conditions, the adrenal glands release corticosteroid hormones into the bloodstream. Corticosteroids combat stress, reduce the excitability of an animal, helping it to face up to adversity, and are also anti-inflammatory and anti-allergic. Crucially, the corticosteroids have another important effect in the context of sex; they feed back to the pituitary gland the necessity of instructing the male testes to pour out more testosterone.

The net effect of all the preceding is that we find a dog that has the broadest life experience as he grows up, and copes well with the accompanying stress levels, becomes a leader in the pack and is rewarded with a rise in the level of his testosterone. That helps him to maintain his dominant position. In short, stress produces corticosteroids. Corticosteroids combat stress and boost testosterone, and testosterone helps maintain dominance and leads to sexual activity.

Testosterone and its effect on behavior

So, instead of the common assumption that high levels of testosterone result in a "macho" dog (or man), we can see that the way in which the stress of life is coped with (the degree of "machismo," if you will) controls the testosterone output. A dog or a man is not born with a high testosterone level that automatically guarantees him a lifetime as top dog. A successful dog (or athlete or businessman) will, as a consequence of that success, have increased testosterone output, which then goes on to help him to maintain his leading position. An underdog—a dog that loses a battle (or an athlete who has failed to win games or a businessman whose firm is doing badly)—will produce lower testosterone levels.

In addition, high levels of sex hormones in the blood affect the behavior of both man and dog. Dogs with high corticosteroid levels have a tendency to be more aggressive and, at puberty, when testosterone levels rise, they can change their patterns of behavior, sometimes dramatically.

The scent of a bitch in heat (estrus) triggers the male dog's brain to signal the pituitary gland, which, in turn, sends a hormone through the bloodstream to the testes, stimulating them to produce more testosterone. But testosterone alone cannot initiate sex. A dog that has not socialized sufficiently may possess plenty of testosterone yet can make a mess of mating. Conversely, a dog that has been castrated and thus lacks testosterone will, if his social development was normal, continue to mate, mounting a bitch as if he were still entire.

Estrogen and its effect on behavior

The ovaries of the bitch are also controlled by the pituitary gland. The latter sets the cycle of ovarian activity. When the point on the cycle is reached that estrus occurs, the ovaries pour out the hormone estrogen. Estrogen influences the behavior of the bitch. She will be "coquettish" and receptive in the presence of a male as well as often being more active and sensitive. Curiously, some bitches act in a masculine way from time to time, mounting other dogs of either sex, or cocking their legs to urinate. Not uncommonly, bitches apparently think and behave as if they were pregnant when this is, in fact, not true. It is a case of the glands bizarrely affecting the canine mind as well as some of the bodily functions. Other species, such as cats and rabbits, sometimes exhibit signs of false pregnancy, and it very occasionally occurs in women. Mary Tudor, Queen of England (1516–1558), was one such.

Other hormonal effects

The brain and its pituitary gland are also involved in controlling many other bodily functions, often as a result of some behavioral or sensory stimulus. A hormone involved in physical development, growth hormone, is released from a puppy's pituitary gland when he takes a nap. The youngster grows while he sleeps, so it is not surprising that puppies sleep more than adult dogs. When the ears of a lactating bitch hear the sound of a newborn puppy crying, they inform the brain, which at once instructs the pituitary gland to release another of its arsenal of hormones, one that lets down milk in the mammary glands.

Glands and domestication

Some fascinating work by Russian scientist Dr. Dimitry Belyaev has thrown light on the role of the glands in the domestication of the dog. Perhaps the most striking thing about domestic dogs (and other domestic animals) is the variety of ways in which they differ physically from their wild relatives. Wolves of any given species all look very much alike.

So it is with wild dogs. Domestic dogs, however, come in all sorts of sizes, colors, coat patterns, head and ear shapes, and so on.

Belyaev speculated that one special feature of the domestication process could be responsible. Perhaps tameness was the single behavioral trait that determined how well the animal adapted to life with human beings. We know that behavior is under the influence of the brain and hormones. Could man's artificial selection over millennia of particular dogs to live and work with him on the basis of their tameness have led to changes in the brain/hormone mechanisms, which in turn affected their bodies in other ways?

Proof of tameness–physical diversity link

Forty years ago Belyaev began experiments in Siberia with foxes to test if his theory could be true. He started with 130 wild foxes and, for generation after generation, selected only the tamest ones to carry on breeding. Now the results dramatically prove him right. The foxes of the latest generation are incredibly tame, unaggressive, and eager to please humans. The corticosteroids in their blood, involved in combating stress situations (see page 29), have dropped to very low levels and the serotonin, a chemical produced by another gland in the brain, the pineal, and which acts as a major player in the mood and emotional functions of the brain, is now at much higher levels than in wild foxes.

What is more, the physical changes in the foxes are like those we see in dogs. They display a range of coat colors, their heads are more compact with a round skull and snub nose, and some have floppy ears! It appears that the gene associated with tameness is, as Belyaev says, the "conductor" of an orchestra of other genes that influence some of the animals' physical features. So, we can now say with confidence that a major reason why Afghan Hounds do not look like Pugs or German Shepherd Dogs is because their ancestors were tame.

Your dog's super senses

Thought, especially of a creative kind, depends on being able to analyze and consider, then act upon incoming information—in fact, one meaning of the word "intelligence" is the obtaining and conveying of information. Animals receive this information through their senses, and the dog in particular is equipped with a range of highly developed, and, in some cases, truly incredible senses. Its "intelligence services" are super efficient and some, about whose mechanisms we know little, might accurately be termed "secret services." These remarkable powers are indeed a facet of the canine's genius, because one dictionary definition of the word "genius" is natural ability, aptitude, and inclination.

Man recognized the value of the acutely tuned senses of the dog when he first began the process of its domestication. Over millennia, as he selectively bred the animal to perform a variety of tasks, it was the canine senses as much as its physical attributes—running speed, alarm barking, and dental weaponry— that he exploited. Here was a working partner for Man the Hunter that could see, hear, or smell far better than he could!

Smell

All dogs are great sniffers, endowed with a sense of smell more acute than that of most other species of animal. Good as they are, Bloodhounds, famous for their exploits in the Sherlock Holmes genre of thrillers, do not do much tracking and security work for us nowadays. Among top canine sniffers of modern times are the Spaniel and the German Shepherd. Probably the most accomplished "sniffing" breed is the Bloodhound.

Its power

Dogs, as we know, have a marvellous sense of smell, with male dogs being better sniffers than bitches. Puppies, born with their eyes closed, depend on their sense of smell, guiding them to their mother and her milk supply to help them survive in their early days of life. (It is thought that newborn puppies also have infrared heat-detecting receptors in their noses to help them do this.) Although it varies from breed to breed and among individuals in any one breed, a dog's olfactory ability is up to a million times better than our own.

Its nature

Domestic dogs can pick up the scent of a chemical at a dilution of one to two parts in a trillion, the equivalent of locating one bad apple in two billion barrels! They can distinguish between individual human odors, even between those of identical twins, provided the two odors are presented together. The odor of one twin would, however, be accepted in place of the other if the latter was not present. Odors from different regions of the body—armpit, palm of hand, sole of foot—although perceptible to man, do not confuse a dog in its

identification of an individual. The canine nostril can detect the smell trace left by human fingerprints on glass for up to six weeks if the glass has been indoors, and for one to two weeks if exposed to the elements outdoors.

Tracking skills

Experiments have shown that the dog can continue tracking individuals across open country even after they have put on gumboots or mounted a bicycle. Scientists think that, on losing the original scent, a dog follows the scent of bruised grass, the only detectable trail.

The dog's close relative, the wolf, also has a nose so finely tuned that it can detect and analyze a three-week-old dried patch of urine from a distance of 330 yd (300 m). Wolves can track prey even when it enters a river or lake, being able to detect the presence of a single drop of blood or urine in 10,000 gallons (45,500 liters) of water, an ability that has been handed down to today's scent hounds.

Scents are best preserved when the ground temperature is a little higher than the air temperature. These conditions usually occur in the early evening, so it is no surprise to learn that this is the favorite hunting time of many of the more keen-scented canid species.

Tracker dogs can recognize the "scent image" of a person, and make deductions from the evaporation and disappearance of various ingredients with time. This allows them to run along a trail for a few feet, register the change in the image, and thus

Smeller rivals

In the animal kingdom, only eels are notably better smellers than dogs, while butterflies are reported to have a sense of smell that is equal in sensitivity to that of the dog, but with the ability to use it at much longer distances.

even determine which way the person was traveling. Coonhounds, those highly specialized trackers not only of raccoons but also deer, bear, and puma, can tell when a scent was laid down, how fast the animal was traveling, and in which direction.

Working "sniffer" dogs

Dogs are used in France and Italy to find the prized truffle fungus that grows up to 12 in (30 cm) underground. Up until a few years ago, there was a University of Truffle Hounds in the town of Roddi near Alba in Italy where dogs were trained in this highly skilled work. In Holland and Denmark, dogs go about the more mundane task of detecting gas leaks. They are more sensitive than the most advanced of odor-measuring machines, and nowadays can be found worldwide helping security services, police and customs officers, and the armed forces to search for explosives, drugs, and people. They are credited with saving hundreds of lives in the conflicts in Iraq and Afghanistan.

When climbers are overwhelmed by avalanches and lie buried under densely packed snow, only rescue dogs can discern the few odor molecules from the victims, which rise to the surface. Recently it has been shown that they can pick out patients with bladder cancer and prostate disease by sniffing samples of their urine, as well as distinguish cancerous melanomas from other less dangerous skin tumors. It seems that they can recognize the specific, incredibly faint odors, undetectable through smell by humans, given off by diseased as opposed to healthy cells.

The newest use of sniffer dogs, mainly English Springer Spaniels, is within the prison service. The dogs have been trained to recognize the apparently distinctive smell, to the canine nostril, of mobile telephones, and are used to search prisoners' cells for these illicit items.

The dog's olfactory system

Smells consist of molecules of particular chemicals floating in the air. When these molecules land on the special olfactory membrane inside a nose, nerve impulses convey the "smell information" to a particular part of the brain, the olfactory center, where it is analyzed. There are 40 times more brain cells involved in scent recognition in the brain of the dog than in our brain.

Olfactory system

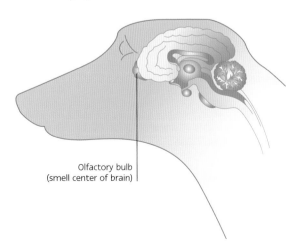

Olfactory bulb
(smell center of brain)

The area of olfactory membrane in the adult human nose is about ½ sq in (3 sq cm), whereas in the average canine nose it covers almost 20 sq in (130 sq cm) being arranged in folds that filter smells from the incoming air. To accommodate such a structure, dogs have developed long noses (with some exceptions among the recent artificially selected breeds). There are also far more sensory cells in the dog's olfactory membrane than in ours. We have about 5 million such cells, a Dachshund 125 million, a Fox Terrier 147 million, and, greatest of sniffers that he is, the German Shepherd Dog 220 million.

Dogs also possess a structure, the vomero-nasal or Jacobson's organ, that is also involved in the detection of smells, particularly pheromones and body odors so important to the animal's sexual and socializing activities. This organ is similar to, but not as large as, the one found in cats. It is a tiny sac lined with receptor cells situated at the front of the roof of the mouth, and opening via a duct into both the mouth and nasal passages.

A wet nose helps in smelling: it dissolves molecules floating in the air, bringing them into close contact with the olfactory membrane, and clears old smells away. Pigment helps too, but how this works is not yet clear. The pigment is not in the sensory cells but nearby; a dog's nasal membranes are dark, and the black pigment in the nose may also play a part in improving the nose-owner's sense of smell, although those dogs that have pink noses seem to sniff perfectly well!

Scent marking

Smell is supremely important to dogs as a medium for communication. Sniffing anything unfamiliar, including other dogs and humans, is one of the dog's strongest instincts. It relies more on smell than sight or sound. Scent marking of territory is as vital to the domestic dog as it is to the wolf in the forest. A urine patch leaves an enduring scent that marks what the dog considers to be, or is claiming as, his territory. Male dogs and wolves have a desire to urinate a small amount frequently for this purpose. Bitches do it as well, but not so noticeably as male dogs.

Similarly, a dog uses the strong-smelling secretion from the sebaceous glands in its anal sacs to put its own personal smell on its droppings. These secretions, so avidly sniffed when dogs meet one another, probably convey a lot of chemical information concerning the bottom-owner's status and other matters, which is utterly unavailable to the human nostril. Another form of scent marking is scratching the ground with the hind paw, kicking up earth (often to his gardening owner's considerable vexation)! This leaves behind the scent produced by sweat glands in the hind paws.

Sometimes dogs apply their own version of "after-shave" by rolling in strong-smelling substances—we assume to reinforce their own body smell. These

Master sniffers

Although Bloodhounds, since the days of Sir Arthur Conan Doyle's famous fictional detective Sherlock Holmes around the turn of the 19th century, have enjoyed the reputation of being the most accomplished sniffers, tests show Miniature Poodles to be just as good! Surprisingly, inhabitants of the Pacific island of Guam reckon Jack Russells to be best at sniffing out snakes and promptly dispatching them.

"fragrances" usually smell terrible to us but not to the dog. So why, if they are such masters of sniffing at long distances, do dogs love to plunge their noses into piles of dung or smell other dogs' bottoms? The answer is we just don't know, but they seem to get a lot of pleasure out of it!

Hearing

Yes, I know, we've all had experience of a dog that apparently isn't listening or cannot hear when you tell him to do something. That is canine contrariness not deafness! In fact dogs have excellent hearing—many times better than that of human beings. And it is their acute sense of hearing, coupled with their intelligence, which enables them to change the lives of profoundly deaf people as Hearing Dogs, in the same way that Guide Dogs assist the blind.

Its power

The sense of hearing of dogs is superb and far more advanced than that of humans. Although some breeds have better hearing than others, most dogs are equipped with large external ears that are served by 17 muscles used to prick and swivel these sound receivers so that they can focus on the source of any noise and locate it within around six one-hundredths of a second. They can register sounds of up to 44,000 waves or cycles per second (as compared to 79,000 per second in cats but only a mere 20,000 per second in man), which means that they detect noises well beyond the range of the human ear, such as those produced by the "silent" dog whistle.

Its nature

Dogs can detect sounds from up to four times the distance that most humans can. In addition, they are sensitive enough to be able to tell the difference between, for example, two metronomes, one ticking at 100 beats per minute and the other at 96. This ability enables a dog to distinguish the sound of his owner's car as it approaches home from all the other vehicles moving in the vicinity. Dogs can also shut off their inner ears to filter from the general din those sounds on which they want to concentrate. Fireworks, however, sound at least five times louder to our pets than they do to us. Dogs do not have as good a sense of hearing as cats, but have a much better sense of smell.

SMART DOG TALE

The acute hearing and intelligence of a blind dog saved the life of a young Canadian woman in November 2005. Samuri, a Japanese Akita, was in the yard of the Drozdowski family home as it became dark. His owners were indoors when Samuri began to bark in an unusual, insistent way they had never heard before. Going outside to investigate, Mr. Drozdowski at first could see nothing, but the dog kept barking and making motions toward the street. There, lying in the gutter, was a woman. She was slipping in and out of consciousness, having suffered a stroke. Her cries were too faint to be heard—except by the blind Samuri. Thanks to him, the ambulance was soon on the scene and the patient taken to hospital, where she recovered.

Sight

Dogs, particulary the "sight hounds" such as the Greyhound, Saluki, and Afghan, have powerful visual abilities that, in some respects, are superior to those of humans. They can see better in dim or flickering light, and they detect the motion of objects far better than we can. They cannot, however, focus as well as us, being only able to see clearly at a distance of 20 ft (6 m) what we can see at 75 ft (23 m). Their color vision is also limited.

Its nature

A dog can see better in the dark than man, partly because the retinas in its eyes have a higher proportion of so-called rod cells that are sensitive to low light levels, and partly because of the shiny *tapetum lucidum* layer (absent in humans but even better developed in cats) that lies underneath the rod cells and reflects light back through them. Dogs can miss seeing objects that are stationary, and, as a consequence, sometimes seem clumsy by blundering into them. This tendency is also influenced by dogs having less stereoscopic vision than man, and thus not being so good at judging distances, though dogs are highly sensitive at seeing moving objects far away. Both these visual faculties are of great value to wild dogs that commonly go hunting in poor light conditions.

How dogs see the world

Dogs do not perceive the world in color as we do. Instead, they see in black, white, shades of gray, and a little blue and yellow, and thus their color appreciation is somewhat similar to that of red-green color-blind people. Unlike us, they do not have much appreciation of visual detail. On the other hand, their brains contain much bigger areas involved in processing scent and motion data than ours do. So, while the good color vision of man and other primates enable them to spot the ripest and most nutritious fruits, canines are equally well adapted as nocturnal hunters of camouflaged prey.

Veterinary opthamologists have found that some dog breeds are more nearsighted than others. These include the German Shepherd, the Schnauzer, and, most nearsighted of all, the Rottweiler.

Other **senses**

Apart from the three major senses of sight, smell, and hearing, dogs possess other more mysterious senses, including some that are barely understood by science. It is likely that dogs can receive information by extrasensory perception (telepathy). However, some of their abilities, such as predicting earthquakes or their owner's return home, may be due to their highly tuned major senses, such as hearing and a sensitivity to vibrations that are undetectable by humans.

Early-warning abilities

Dogs (and cats) are very sensitive to vibrations, and will give warning of volcanic eruptions and earthquakes some considerable time, occasionally even days, before humans are aware of any movement. Villagers living on the slopes of dormant volcanoes, such as Mount Etna in Sicily, know that when their pets suddenly dash out of the house for no apparent reason, it is wise to follow them. Dogs are reported to have behaved in similar fashion when the tsunami struck in Indonesia in December 2004. Curiously, dogs react like this only to the imminence of the "real thing" and not to the 150,000 other harmless vibrations of the Earth's crust that occur each year and apparently do not alarm them. Some scientists hold a different view of canine earthquake prediction. They believe that the animals detect electrostatic changes in the atmosphere that are known to precede certain earthquakes and volcanic eruptions.

Some dogs are born with a mysterious ability to detect an oncoming epileptic seizure in a human being minutes or even hours before it occurs. Others sense and warn of a dangerous rise in their owner's blood pressure. We just do not know how they do it. So-called seizure alert dogs are now being provided to epilepsy sufferers in some countries. The dogs warn of the impending attack by anxious barking, whining or pawing, which attracts the attention of patients, allowing them to find a safe place to lie down and wait for the episodes to pass. Some of these dogs automatically stay close to the patient when the attack occurs, perhaps licking the person's face or hands; other seizure alert dogs have been trained to do so and, in some cases, to press a button on the telephone that informs the emergency services. Dogs cannot, however, be *trained* to alert seizures. They are either born with this remarkable gift or not—another aspect of canine genius.

Touch

The sense of touch is very important to dogs. Like us, their body skin contains large numbers of touch-sensitive nerve endings. To a newborn puppy, the touch of his mother is immensely comforting and soothing, and when he is older, touch continues to please and reassure. Stroking your dog is in itself a reward and act of bonding for the pet; stroking not only lowers *his* heart rate and blood pressure, but does the same for you too! The canine body carries a number of specialized touch-sensitive hairs, vibrissae or whiskers on various parts of the body, most importantly the muzzle. These hairs, linked to large sensory nerve endings and well supplied with blood, help the dog explore its environment, investigate objects, and detect currents of air.

Taste

The dog's sense of taste is relatively poorly developed compared with man's. This is probably because, unlike man's vegetarian primate ancestors that could select from a range of food in front of them, the wolves and wild dogs that gave rise to domestic dogs were carnivores that spotted their prey at a distance and had to eat what they could catch. Whereas humans have some 9,000 taste buds on their tongues, dogs have only around 1,700. As with us, these taste buds can register "sweet," "sour," "bitter," and "salty." They also appear to have one that registers "water." This

latter may be the reason why some dogs seem as discerning about water sources as wine buffs are about clarets and burgundies. No doubt you have witnessed the dog for which you have just put down a bowl of sparkling fresh water go straight off and drink from the muddy puddle in the garden. There must be some flavor in the water that makes it more attractive to the canine palate than the chemically purified version that comes out of the tap, but we just don't know what it is. Alternatively, dogs may be simply showing their dislike of the frequently distinct chlorine taste and smell of the domestic water supply.

Overall, however, taste is not as important to carnivores such as dogs as it is to omnivorous human beings. To dogs, when choosing to eat, smell comes first, then texture, and, lastly, taste.

A sixth sense?

There is much debate about whether dogs possess another type of sense, a "sixth sense," or rather extrasensory perception. In 1952, the CIA tried to enlist dogs with extrasensory perception abilities for spying duties, although there is no recorded evidence of their success. But are they telepathic? According to surveys, 48 percent of owners in the U.S. and England believe their dogs have this ability, and that they do respond to unspoken commands and thoughts.

Of course, the frequently mentioned cases of dogs that know when their owners are on the way home from work; when, much to their distaste, they are due to visit the veterinarian, or when they are about to be taken for a walk can be often explained without taking telepathy into account. As explained earlier, a dog's acute sense of hearing can recognize the sound of a familiar car engine when it is still a long distance away (see page 38), and the owner's preparatory behavior and words, spoken to another human being and not directly to the dog, when planning a walk can be quickly picked up by these highly perceptive creatures. They are far more sensitive to the slightest nuances of our moods,

and behavior than you might think, and they do recognize an extensive vocabulary of human words, including in many cases their meanings, even though they cannot speak them (see page 98).

Scientific evidence of canine ESP

Nevertheless, there is strong evidence, based on well-conducted scientific experiments, that dogs are truly telepathic. Dr. Rupert Sheldrake, a biochemist and investigator of the paranormal, has described his findings while studying Jaytee, a terrier living in Lancashire, England. He found that the dog went to the window every weekday at around 4.30 pm when his mistress left her workplace some 14 miles (22 km) away, and sat there until she arrived approximately 45 minutes later.

Sheldrake carried out over 100 experiments with Jaytee, including many supervised by "sceptics." In some, the owner varied the time she set off back from work without informing her family so that they could not subconsciously give the dog cues. To eliminate the "familiar car sound" factor, she sometimes traveled back by unfamiliar means, such as bicycle, taxi, or train. In *every* case, Jaytee started sitting at the window at the time the owner set off for home. The odds against this being a chance effect are more than 100,000 to one.

Sheldrake also carried out a survey among pet owners in Greater Manchester and found that 46 percent of dog owners, as compared to 14 percent of cat owners, claimed that their animals somehow knew in advance when a member of the family was on the way home.

Routine perception

Jaytee's intriguing ability is quite different from the situation commonly remarked upon by owners whereby their pets anticipate their return home from work. Some dogs will begin pacing around, whining, and visiting the front door up to 30 minutes before the owner is expected. This behavior proves that dogs have a highly accurate sense of time and daily routine in their surroundings, *not* that they are necessarily very intelligent, and it is only a sense of the *daily* routine —they have no concept of a week. This is why they continue to go through the same performance at weekends when the owner is not at work.

Certainly, dogs possess association skills and are capable of linking two ideas in their minds. The Russian scientist Pavlov famously demonstrated at the end of the 19th century the ability of dogs to associate the sound of a ringing bell with feeding time. They cannot, however, associate events that are separated in time, which is why, if your dog runs off when you are out for a walk and returns two hours later, it is futile to punish him. He cannot comprehend that the punishment was for something he did hours ago.

Sensing human emotion

Some people believe that it is possible for a human being to communicate with a dog or other species of pet telepathically, and there are so-called animal psychics who claim to do this professionally. In terms of purely anecdotal evidence, working as a veterinarian with a wide range of animals,

Canine empathy?

The well-known American author, anthropologist, and animal lover Elizabeth Marshall Thomas in her book *The Hidden Life of Dogs* (see page 140) described her pet dog's "empathetic observation" when, on one occasion, he "assessed my mood, which was dark, over a distance of about one hundred yards, and changed his demeanor from cheery to bleak in response." Some animal psychologists and certainly all dog whisperers (see page 54) would disagree with Ms. Thomas's claim of canine empathy, explaining the animal's behavior as being simply in response to her "negative" body language, with no mind-reading involved.

particularly wild exotic ones, including wolves and wild dogs, but also with domestic pets, when I was in a positive, wholly optimistic mood, it somehow transmitted to my patients. If I felt really upbeat, they seemed to respond quickly and well to my ministrations and recover; whereas when I was in a negative frame of mind, they did not. It may have been that a change in body odor was involved or that it was a matter of mental communication; there is no way of knowing.

More than any other type of domesticated animal, dogs display through their vocalizations, body language, behavior, and facial expressions a range of complex, humanlike emotions, including anger, happiness, anxiety, and surprise. There is also no doubt that they can feel pangs of jealousy as, for example, when their owner becomes involved with some other person or animal. There is one infamous case of a pair of male Boxers who apparently fell in love with the newly-arrived fiancée of their owner and, like rival human suitors, vied to be her favorite, with the result that bouts of fighting started to occur. The situation was only rectified when the dogs were prescribed a drug to raise the level of serotonin, a major chemical player in mood and emotional functions of the brain.

Navigational skills

There are numerous accounts of dogs (and cats) finding their way home over incredibly long distances. One of the most famous concerns Bobbie, the Wonder Dog of Oregon. In 1923, this Border Collie took six months to find his way back to Silverton, Oregon, from Indiana, where he went missing when taken on a visit by his owners. It was a journey of some 2,550 miles (4,100 km). Each year the town of Silverton still celebrates Bobbie by holding Bobbie Day on February 15, the day the dog arrived back. Another dog, Bear, a Labrador/Chow cross belonging to a family in Wichita, Kansas, took even longer to find his way home. He made it after six years!

But how do such dogs achieve these amazing feats? We are not sure. Suggested mechanisms include celestial navigation, the dog noting the angle of the sun at a certain time of day and subconsciously comparing it with the angle it would be at the same time over his home. Noting a difference, the dog might move in a certain direction, check the sun again and, finding the angle "worse," change course. When the angle improved, this would indicate the "right" direction. Of course, dogs do not wear watches to give them the time, but it seems probable that, in common with man and the higher mammals (and cockroaches!), they do possess internal biological clocks. Another possibility is that the canine brain, like that of the pigeon, contains magnetically sensitive cells, which act as internal compasses.

Over much shorter distances than that trekked by Bobbie, dogs find their way home using a cognitive map of the home range area, which they have stored in their brains during all their previous wanderings. This map represents a record of how key points in the environment are geometrically related, and it enables the dog, like humans, bees, and turtles, to take the shortest route home once they have located the target destination.

Dreaming

Dogs sleep on average for about half of the day, stand for about a quarter of it, and lie or sit down for the remaining quarter. Some of the larger breeds of dog, such as the Newfoundland, St. Bernard, and Mastiff, regularly sleep for 16 to 18 hours each day. Do they dream? Owners, having observed their pet lying on the hearthrug paddling away with his legs, twitching his lips, and perhaps vocalizing while clearly asleep, believe so. Rapid eye movement (REM) sleep in humans is associated with dreaming, and similar REM sleep with movement of the eyeballs is seen in dogs. In both humans and dogs, when they go to sleep, first comes slow wave sleep (SWS), where brain waves are slow and, while muscles are not completely relaxed, the brain is at its most restful. Then follows the REM sleep period.

SMART DOG TALE

A few years ago, a lady in Inverness, Scotland, sent her Border Collie to live with a friend in Calcutta, India. Some months later, the dog suddenly turned up again at its old home in Inverness! Apparently he had boarded a ship in Calcutta that was bound for Dundee. Once there, he transferred to a coastal vessel sailing to Inverness. How do we pigeonhole that example of genius? Inexplicable. At the time it was said that the dog was attracted by the familiar, Scottish accent of crew members on the ship.

Puppies spend more time in REM sleep than adult dogs probably because, during the day, they are learning all manner of new things, and, later, when it's sleep time, the brain has to digest, process, and file away all the accumulated information. We can only guess, however what they actually dream about and whether they have powers of imagination to go with those dreams.

Dreaming in both man and dog seems to be necessary for the routine processing and data storage of memories gathered during the day. The memory banks of the brain need purging and reorganizing during sleep, a procedure that we call dreaming.

Of course, we can only imagine what dogs may dream about, and there is no way of finding out the answer to the frequently asked question "Do they dream in colour?" When dogs are asleep and apparently dreaming, they move much more than most dreaming humans. They dream for shorter periods of time than we do, with puppies dreaming more than old dogs and small dog breeds more than big breeds. Even if a sleeping dog appears to be having a nightmare, it is best not to wake it up.

Communicating
with your dog

Dogs are unable to use true speech to express their feelings, but, being fairly vocal animals, emitting a repertoire of sounds ranging from barks and growls of varying intensity to whimpers and whines, they can use their voices to "speak" and express themselves. However, the most important method of communication used by dogs over short distances is body language, and, as a dog owner, it is important that you should be able to read these signals.

As we cannot converse with our pets using a language of words, the innovative technique of dog whispering can show how to communicate man to dog and dog to man in other ways. This gentle, utterly humane, psychological, almost in some ways spiritual, approach enables us to appreciate other aspects of the canine genius.

Other remarkable aspects of the dog's mind are its powers of memory and of calculation, the latter involving some mathematical ability and even a degree of geometrical skill in working out spatial problems—an ability particularly valuable to pastoral and working breeds of dog (see pages 66–67 and 76–77).

Vocalizaton

Some years ago a dog appeared on television that could utter, to the great amusement of audiences, the word "sausages." We are not concerned with such things here. The vocalization we are about to consider is no trick trained for the stage, but the normal language of the dog—the vocabulary of barks and other sounds that it uses, often along with other methods of communication, to express emotions and to convey messages.

Using pitch and volume

By raising the pitch or volume of their barks, dogs can indicate frustration or emotion. Researchers at the University of California have studied the vocalizations of ten dogs from six breeds and found that their barks varied according to the situation. For example, a high-pitched bark seemed to say "Where is my owner?" while a lower-pitched, harsher one meant "A stranger is coming!"

Growling is more often aggressive in adult dogs than puppies. Some dogs "play growl," where a mock growl is emitted when they are "teasing." A rolling sound, rather like a growl but fluctuating in pitch, can be considered nonaggressive. Aggressive growls have either a constant or steadily rising pitch, and are accompanied by aggressive body language (see page 52).

Talking to us

The vocalization of dogs has evolved into a sort of language as an accompaniment to and consequence of the process of canine domestication, a process more intimate than the domestication of other animals, such as the horse, cow, or cat. They and we now share a society in which interspecies communication skills are invaluable. Ethologists at the Eotvos Lorand University in Hungary played recordings of the barkings of Hungarian Mudis, a pastoral breed (see pages 66–67), to some 90 human volunteers. The recordings were of the dogs vocalizing in various situations, such as encountering an intruder, anticipating a meal, and playing with other dogs. Irrespective of whether they had ever owned a Mudi or not, the people were remarkably accurate at identifying the emotional meaning of the various barks and the situations that brought them about. They were correct in one out of three situations, which is double the rate to be expected when guessing by chance. Therefore, it can be said that, in a sense, dogs are learning to talk to us.

Aid to translating canine

But now, for the owner or dog who has everything, the Japanese have come up with what they consider to be the ultimate aid to communication between man and dog—a gizmo called Bowlingual, which the Tokyo-based Takara company claims can translate dogs' barks, whines, and woofs into words or phrases in the owner's language. It consists of a 3 in (7.5 cm) microphone attached to the dog's collar transmitting sounds to a palm-sized console containing a database. The console recognizes six emotional categories of dog "voice"— happiness, sadness, frustration, anger, assertion, and desire. "Grrooof!" or "Yowooo!" goes the dog and out of the machine comes "You're telling me off!," "That was fun!" or "I'm *still* waiting patiently."

Body language

In both humans and dogs, communication through body language, sometimes subtle, sometimes obvious, is a feature of normal behavior. It can be done either consciously or unconsciously by both species and, of course, it is designed to be picked up by the eyes of the observers to whom it is directed. While speech is more important to humans, body language and smell are key to canine communication.

Learning your dog's body signals

Every dog has a comprehensive range of "body signals" that it can use to express its emotions and intentions. These can involve the whole body or parts of it, including facial expressions, and may frequently be accompanied by some form of vocalization. Be alert and "tuned in" to recognize signs based on body posture, vocalization, ears, eyes, lips, tongue, tail, and body hair.

The normal dog

The "normal" dog, happy and alert, carries its tail well with no tension in its body. It moves freely and holds its head high. The tongue may loll out and the jaws are relaxed.

Wanting to play

A dog in a playful mood often dips down at the front into a crouch, the back bowed. It gives little barks or rolling growls with high notes. It may raise one forefoot and lean to one side, its head almost on the ground or jump backwards or forwards, the head looking up with relaxed jaws. The tail wags.

Submission

Here the dog adopts a lower crouch and may raise its forefeet in mild play invitation. The teeth are not on view, there is no tension in the body, and, usually, there is no vocalization. As it crouches lower, it may lick a little. A submissive dog often turns side-on to present its flank. The ears are folded back.

Complete submission

The dog's ears are folded down and the tail is dropped and folded around one leg or, with very nervous animals, tucked right under the body. The head is down to avoid eye contact (with reassurance it comes up). The final stage in submission is rolling over with one hind leg raised. Unless fearful, the dog usually raises its ears a little to indicate that its submission stems from trust.

Fearful aggression

This occurs when the dog is faced with a threat. Here the dog shows his teeth and emits a constant low growl or snarl, or even barks. The ears are laid back and the tail is held down and rigid. The whole body is tense, with the hind legs braced ready for rapid movement. The hair down the center of the dog's back stands on end.

Dominant aggression

This is seen when the dog is instigating a confrontation. Rather than simply warning off its opponent, the dog advances confidently with tail and ears held high. It looks directly and unblinking at the target, with teeth bared and, in most cases, snapping.

Tail wagging

Recent research from Italy has found that whether dogs wag their tails to the left or right depends on their emotions at the time. Wagging to the right is normally a sign that the dog is relaxed and in a good mood. Wagging to the left suggests the animal is uncertain, apprehensive, and considering departing the scene. As with humans, the right side of the canine brain controls the left side of the body and is associated with retreat behavior, while the left side controls the right side of the body and is associated with a happy disposition.

Facial expressions

Like ourselves, dogs are equipped with facial muscles capable of creating different expressions of the face, although these muscles are not nearly as numerous or efficiently controlled as man's.

The lips can be curled back to expose the animal's weaponry, its teeth. Baring the teeth is not always aggressive—some dogs seem almost to laugh and, when very pleased, their lips are drawn back to expose the incisors (front) teeth. In aggression, the lips are drawn back further, often exposing the pointed canine (fang) teeth.

The ears are extremely mobile and can turn to follow sounds—even drop-eared dogs such as spaniels can move their ears into an alert position, although they do not have the range of expression of those breeds with erect ears.

The eyes are also very expressive. When a dog is happy, there is a brightening of the eyes. Some dogs raise their eyelids and eyebrows when surprised or quizzical—this is often exaggerated by a tilting of the head. In fearful aggression, the dog may present a wild, wide-eyed look with the facial skin drawn back, whites of the eyes exposed, and pupils dilated. In dominant aggression, the pupils are

constricted as the dog stares fixedly at its opponent, daring eye contact. To a dog, a fixed stare is a challenge. Usually a person staring at a dog will cause it to look away and become submissive. A dog sure of itself and of its relationship with its owner may simply react with a questioning look. Nevertheless, don't try to "stare out" a dog unless you are confident you can handle the potential attack that may follow you losing this contest!

The talking tail

A dog's tail is an integral part of the animal's communications system, as well as being used for balancing and, when swimming, as a rudder. The dog wags his tail to show pleasure or as an invitation to play or come for a walk. It can be held low and straight out as part of an aggression display or tucked under in fear and submission (see pages 51–52). One of the undesirable results of the totally unnecessary mutilation of a dog that we call docking is that the docked dog cannot easily signal submission and consequently could end up in an unwanted fight. It may well be that the original reason for docking fighting breeds of dogs, such as

Dobermann Pinschers and Rottweilers, was exactly that: to stimulate aggression by preventing adequate expression of submission.

Professor Coren (see page 18) has investigated the dog's "tail language" in great detail and claims to be able to recognize the meaning of subtle differences in the tail's position or movement. Here are some of his conclusions:

- A broad tail wag means "I like you."
- A slight tail wag means "I see you looking at me. You like me, don't you?"
- A slow tail wag with the tail at half-mast means "I want to know what you mean, but I just can't figure it out."
- A tail held almost horizontal, pointing away from the body but not stiff, is saying "Something interesting may be happening here."
- A tail held up and slightly curved over the back is declaring "I am top dog!"
- A tail that is down near the hind legs with the legs bent slightly inwards is indicating "I'm feeling a bit insecure."

Dog **whispering**

Dog whispering is a fairly recent technique of interaction between dog and man that can be used as a method of training, or simply to allow an owner to relate more closely to his pet by imitating its body language. So you want to understand your dog? Then you might have to start acting like a dog! As well as deepening the relationship between man and dog, a basic understanding of dog whispering makes the training of a pet progress faster, increases the range of the dog's potential abilities, and gives added pleasure and satisfaction to the dog-loving owner.

Basic principles

First there was horse whispering, made famous by Robert Redford's film, *The Horse Whisperer*, and then came dog whispering. By no means a newfangled fad of doting dog lovers but a revolutionary technique based on the science of canine ethology, the study of dog behavior under natural conditions, dog whispering develops the mutual understanding of feelings and needs between dog and owner. Its core principle is the establishment of a "pack" relationship between dog and owner, in which the owner is pack leader or alpha dog. Dogs, even the most pampered pedigree Papillon or Chihuahua, inherently "understand" the pack-organized way of life. It is in their genes.

Dog whispering can be used purely to enhance and deepen the relationship between a dog and its owner or as an actual training technique that does not involve formal training, leads, and so on. It can form an invaluable part of the overall training of a dog, enabling the owner to "read" a pet's feelings and attitudes, but by itself it cannot teach obedience.

Canine calming signals

One of the foremost proponents of dog whispering is the Norwegian Turid Rugaas, who studied wolves and dogs, and found that these animals employ 29 different calming signals of body posture, facial expression, or action to avoid conflict. These include yawning (see page 55), tail wagging, blinking, sniffing the ground, and turning away—behaviors that are often misinterpreted as acts of disobedience or at least disinterest by owners.

Not simply a sign of happiness, tail wagging means that the dog wants to engage at a time when he is happy. Some dogs will wag their tails when being held back from pursuing cats with which they would like to engage or when they are about to engage with intruders. A dog baring its teeth may be in threatening mode, but if the curled-back lips and exposed array of teeth are accompanied by a lowered head and tail, squinting eyes, and low-slouching body, the animal is putting on a display of profound respect and submission.

Your body signals

So, what about human body language as interpreted by the dog? Some threatening human signals are complete stillness, direct, unblinking eye contact, facing the dog directly, deep guttural sounds, and movements over the top of the dog. On the other hand, nonthreatening human signals include squinting, exaggerated blinking, moving from side to side laterally, avoiding direct eye contact, standing parallel to the dog, touching under the chin, taking up a position lower than the dog by squatting, kneeling, and so on, and high-pitched sounds.

Using dog-whispering techniques, how would one deal with an aggressive dog? You must blink, turn away, and stand still. However, it may be going too far to get down on your knees and start sniffing the ground like dogs do!

It should be remembered in all this that dogs are masters of body language and can detect even the slightest movement about eight times better than we can. Dogs are acutely aware of what you are doing—the faint flick of an eyelid, a brief flinching or hesitant gesture, the rate and depth of your breathing. You may think you can hide a feeling of fear or surprise, but these ultrasensitive creatures will detect it. Even if you really are not *acting* scared, a dog will know, because it can smell the pheromones in the perspiration released when a human being is frightened. No human nostril can do that.

Putting simple dog whispering body language into practice will allow you to approach a strange dog, particularly a nervous type, without being snapped at and perhaps bitten.

Do not move toward the dog head on, but from the side. Do not stare fixedly at it. Act slowly and nonchalantly and toss it a tidbit. If it is very nervous, turn your back on the dog and squat down. Put out a hand for it to sniff. Pet it gently if it seems amenable, but do not insist on petting it if it growls or snaps. Take hold of the collar with slow, steady movements of your hand.

Children, with their sudden, erratic movements and tendency to emit high-pitched squeals, are not good at doing these things and need constant supervision when showing an interest in a dog that does not know them.

The meaning of yawning

Dogs do not yawn like we do out of tiredness or boredom. Rather, a canine yawn is, in most cases, a rather placatory gesture, usually on the part of a more dominant individual toward a lesser one, which signifies "Don't worry, I mean you no harm." It can also be a sign of uneasiness or anxiety.

The **mathematical** dog

Research has shown that dogs do have an elementary understanding of numbers, simple addition and subtraction, and can even exhibit an innate ability for trigonometrical calculation. An ability to count is valuable to members of the dog family, particularly when out hunting as a pack. The apparent inbuilt trigonometrical skills are astounding. helping them to perform efficiently and with economy of physical effort.

Canine counting capability

Can a dog count, add and subtract? Other animals, such as birds and rodents, can recognize one pile of objects as being bigger than another, but that is not the same as counting. For the ancestors of our domestic dogs, wolves and wild dogs, pack-living species whose brains contain a big neocortex, the center of reasoning, an ability to count would seem to be valuable, perhaps vital, both within the pack and when out hunting. The animals can note the numbers of allies and enemies in a social gathering and calculate the numbers of prey and fellow hunters when out on the chase. Counting capability must certainly contribute to overall canine intelligence and be an important component of the special talents of pastoral breeds such as the collies, the Australian Kelpie, and, in former times, the working Corgi (see pages 66–67).

Research evidence

Recently, experiments similar to those employed to show that five-month-old babies can count have been applied to dogs. In the baby tests, a number of toy dolls were placed in front of a baby and then a screen raised to hide them from its view. The baby watched as a number of dolls were added or taken, the experimenter's hand dipping behind the screen. Then the screen was removed. If the experimenter had surreptitiously added or taken away a doll and the numbers didn't "add up" for it, the baby stared for much longer than it did if the number of dolls was "right." Presumably, the baby had done calculations and taken into account the experimenter's apparent additions or subtractions, but the resultant number of dolls contradicted expectations.

When this experiment was done using 11 mongrel dogs and dog treats instead of dolls, the dogs reacted in the same way, staring at the bowl of treats for much longer if their sums did not add up. The dogs seemed unconcerned when one treat plus one treat came, as all reasonable dogs and people know, to an expected total of two treats, but when one treat plus one treat apparently equaled three, they were clearly confused. It is thought that, like many mammals, they may be able to count as high as seven.

DIY testing

You can try repeating this experiment with your dog. I tried it with a friend's Labrador Retriever, and one extremely partial to cubes of cheese, which we therefore used as the treats. We did it 25 times, "cheating" the dog by adding or subtracting on seven of them and carefully noting down the duration of gaze. Our results were striking; the dog stared two to three times as long when the numbers were "wrong" and we ended up with a rather contented dog burping strong odors of Cheddar!

Canine performers

Apparently highly numerate performing dogs are sometimes seen in circuses and variety shows, but in almost all cases trickery is involved. For example, the dog rings the bell when a certain number has been reached by responding to some sort of inconspicuous visual signal (the sharp vision of the animal coming into play again), often the slight flick of a little finger given by the handler, and which the audience, not as sharp-sighted as the dog and further away, cannot see.

Canine calculus

Beyond the simple mathematics of addition and subtraction, there is now evidence that dogs have natural abilities in the more advanced field of calculus, that bane of many a schoolchild's maths lessons.

In 2003, Tim Pennings, a mathematician at Hope College, Michigan, noted that when he, as he frequently did, took his Corgi Elvis to the beach and played the game of "Fetch," throwing a tennis ball out into the waves and waiting for Elvis to retrieve it, the dog always took the optimal path, on land and then in the water, which minimized total travel time. If the ball was thrown at an angle to the shoreline, Elvis had several options: to run along the beach until he was directly opposite the ball and then swim out to get it, to plunge in and swim to the ball right away, or to run part of the way along the beach and then enter the water.

Armed with stopwatch and measuring tape, Dr. Pennings carried out repeated ball-retrieving experiments with Elvis and found that, no matter which option the dog chose on a particular occasion and whatever his running and swimming speeds were, the time it took to get to the ball was always the minimum. The mathematician was then surprised to discover that Elvis's performance closely matched a calculus-based model of the situation. The dog's choice of route was identical to the theoretically ideal one on every occasion.

Several other researchers have since confirmed these findings, including two Frenchmen playing "Fetch" with a Labrador Retriever bitch called Salsa on a lakeside beach near Nîmes in Provence, France.

Innate calculating ability

Some scientists think the dog must be able automatically to make instantaneous calculations estimating his speed of approach, both when running and swimming, and at each point in time choose the path giving it maximum speed of approach. Dr. Pennings, on the other hand, as a

result of further experiments with Elvis, believes that a dog forms a "global" decision at the outset as to what is the best path to take. Certainly, this uncanny knack is not learned by our dogs, but is natural and inbuilt, thus demonstrating another facet of the canine genius, and one that must be particularly valuable to the pastoral breeds in their work with moving objects in the form of sheep, cattle, and so on (see pages 66–67). We human beings cannot do it unless sitting at a desk with graph paper, compasses, calculator, and protractor.

You can observe some of the same ability in your pet when throwing a ball or a Frisbee for it to catch. To leap and take it in midair so neatly means that it has calculated the speed, distance, and height of the object in an instant.

Canine **memory**

Dog owners sometimes fret that their pets will perhaps forget them when put in kennels for a period. Dogs do have a memory, but it seems to be different from that of humans, and it is certainly difficult to devise experiments to measure canine powers of recollection. Their memory clearly functions well in everyday life. They recognize family and friends, and are only too aware what it signifies when their owners put on their coats and fetch the leads.

Different types

As with man and other animals, scientists recognize several different areas of canine memory, as detailed in the chart below.

How and what dogs remember

While event memory certainly exists in dogs, it would be difficult to set up an experiment to test a pet for it. It seems most unlikely that it can recall and go over an item stored in its memory at will, but that it must be evoked by some sort of associated stimulus, noted subconsciously as related to a particular smell, sound, or to a pleasant or unpleasant feeling.

Some dog psychologists think that, when an owner goes on vacation, boarding his pet in an unknown kennel, the animal loses all memory of him or her as completely as if he or she never existed. The dog will feel totally abandoned, without recognizable territory of its own and without any pack to belong to. Certain dogs, particularly the more sensitive types, may become severely depressed. Those that are very close to their owners may lapse into listless rejection of all food for several days. When the owner returns from holiday, the pet's memory is triggered by familiar sounds, smells, and sights, and consequently, in a sense, the person comes into existence once more. To put it another way: dogs do not think about their owners when separated from them.

Differences between individuals

Other experts consider that, when a dog has been separated from its owner for over ten hours, the animal's feelings of rejection and desperation fade away, along with the image of the owner in its mind. Judging by the many dogs I have known, I am personally not convinced of this.

Some dogs placed with new owners do settle down contentedly, but there are those, clearly carrying powerful long-term memories, that reject a new home, repeatedly run away, and often actually look sad. It would seem that some dogs get more closely attached to their owners than others and find it difficult or even impossible to accept change, while others, more easy-going and less possessive types, can adapt relatively easily. Genetic factors and innate predispositions may be at the root of it. We just don't know.

Main areas of canine memory

MEMORY AREA	TYPE OF MEMORY
Event memory	Remembering events that have occurred
Semantic memory	Remembering facts
Motor memory	Remembering movement (e.g., how to catch something)
Spatial memory	Remembering places and carrying mental maps of home territory
Social memory	Remembering which person or other animal has been friendly and which not

Limitations in canine thinking

The dog probably cannot think in the sense of musing or reflecting. His memory is not turned on voluntarily, but comes into play only when triggered by some form of stimulus. That is not to say that dogs cannot feel things emotionally (see page 26). They plainly can. You and I don't have to *think* about feeling, say, miserable, and neither do they. Just as some people are sunny by nature and others negative, so it is with our canine companions.

Long-term and short-term memory

This is another way of classifying memory, although the division between the two is often blurred and the subject of much controversy among scientists (mainly because memory testing is so easy in humans and so difficult in other species). Short-term memory is the storage for short periods of "one-off," transient experiences. Long-term memory involves storage of experiences of more fundamental significance in the life of the individual. Dogs aren't very good at remembering in the short term. Some researchers at the University of Michigan, claim that a dog's short-term memory is no longer than five minutes, as compared with 16 hours for the cat. Felines even outdo the monkey and orangutan in this respect! (At the other end of the scale comes the goldfish, which can remember things for all of three seconds.) Rico—see opposite—clearly uses his long-term memory for toy spotting.

Wild characteristics

Despite the great changes that domestication has brought about in the ways in which dogs think and behave, there is still an awful lot of wolf in them, even in the fanciest pedigree breed. In the 1960s, a German scientist, Dr. Zimen, studied and compared the behavior of a pack of wolves and a large group of Poodles kept in adjoining enclosures. He found that the wolves exhibited 362 distinct behaviors, 64 percent of which were exhibited in identical or at least very similar form by the Poodles. Only 13 percent of wolf behaviors, mainly to do with vocal and visual communication, were no longer present in any form in the dogs.

Problem behavior

When it comes to learning to understand their dogs, many owners would dearly like to know the reason why things go wrong and their pets begin to indulge in some kind of undesirable activity. Why has the dog become, for example, aggressive, destructive, unduly excitable, unruly, or prone to toilet troubles? There is no easy answer because there is a whole range of causes, both psychological and environmental, lying behind these behavioral phenomena, some involving the owner, others not.

SMART DOG TALE

Rico is a 13-year-old Border Collie living in Germany. Scientists at the prestigious Max Planck Institute have tested this dog and found that he can recognize the names of over 200 of his toys. Call out the name of the toy and Rico will fetch the correct item 93 percent of the time. What is even more fascinating is his ability to find a toy with which he is *not* familiar. Put a new toy among his collection of well-known ones, call out its name, and Rico will root through them until he finds the unknown item. This shows that he is employing simple logic. He knows that familiar words are associated with familiar objects. Therefore, a strange word must be associated with a strange object.

After one month Rico can still remember the name of the new toy, identifying it correctly around 50 percent of times he is tested, even though he has not been shown it in the meanwhile. This so-called "fast-mapping" behavior allows the experts to equate Rico's learning ability with that of a three-year-old child.

Smart breeds and mongrels

Dog breeds are divided into several major groups, mainly on the basis of the work they originally did, or do, for man. These are recognized by most national Kennel Clubs as Hounds, Pastoral Dogs, Terriers, Utility Dogs, Working Dogs, Toy Dogs, and Gundogs, but with some minor differences. In the U.S., for example, Gundogs are known as Sporting Dogs, while Nonsporting Dogs are roughly equivalent to Utility Dogs and Herding Dogs to Pastoral Dogs. There is also an additional group for Miscellaneous Dogs, for those breeds that have not yet been granted full recognition by the American Kennel Club (AKC). The placing of breeds within groups can also vary from country to country. And then we have that most popular and numerous dog group of all—the mongrels.

Each of these main breed groups is profiled here, including the origins of the dog types, and general characteristics of the present-day breeds. A focus on some of the notable breeds, together with practical strategies on how to improve their intelligence is also included here. The results of Professor Stanley Coren's study of 79 breeds and their understanding of and obedience to commands (see page 18) is then used as a guide to comparative intelligence of specific breeds within each group.

The **hound** family

The athletes of the dog world, these breeds are certainly not for the housebound or those dwelling in high rise city apartments. They need abundant exercise and will certainly provide a lot of exercise for their owners!

Origins

Hounds were the earliest hunting dogs, used by man in the Middle East many thousands of years ago. These Greyhoundlike sight hounds or "gaze-hounds" were swift and silent sprinters. Many centuries later, hounds that tracked game by ground scents were developed in Europe. Typically, these dogs had, like their present-day counterparts, strong, sturdy legs, long heads with long nostrils, pendulous ears, and a remarkable sense of smell—up to one million times better than a human's.

European hound breeds date back at least to the 11th century. One type, the St Hubert, was found in France before 1066, and it is probable that William the Conqueror brought examples of this dog with him when he invaded Britain, thereby introducing bloodlines that still persist in modern breeds, including the Bloodhound.

During the Middle Ages, the landed gentry were mainly responsible for the development of different hound breeds designed to tackle various kinds of quarry, among them the now-extinct Devon

Staghound and the Elkhound for deer and other large species, the Dachshund for badgers, the Beagle for hare, the Coonhound for raccoons, and the Basset Griffon Vendéen for wolves and wild boar.

General characteristics

Athleticism and a wonderful sense of smell are the two great features of this group, and a hound may possess one or both of them. Hounds are practical types, clever at doing things useful to man and which man cannot do anything like as well by himself. Nevertheless, many experts consider hounds as being rather difficult to train.

Individual breeds

Some 34 different hound breeds are recognized today. Apart from employing either sight or smell as their principal hunting aids, some hounds are even more specialized in techniques of working with their human handlers. The Coonhound pursues a raccoon by scent, "trees" its quarry, and then informs the hunter trailing far behind what has happened by altering the tone of its voice and baying distinctively. The Dachshund often seems more like a sprightly

Intelligence	Breed
Above Average Group	Norwegian Elkhound (36)
Average Group	Irish Wolfhound (41); Black and Tan Coonhound (44); English Foxhound, American Foxhound, Otter Hound, Greyhound (46); Scottish Deerhound (47); Dachshund (49); Rhodesian Ridgeback (52); Ibizan Hound (53)
Fair Group	Italian Greyhound (60); Petit Basset Griffon Vendeen (62)
Lowest Group	Basset Hound (71); Bloodhound (74); Afghan Hound (79)

terrier, so happy is it to go underground to confront rabbits, foxes, and, of course, badgers with remarkable tenacity. Hounds are particularly keen on search games.

Comparative intelligence

In Professor Stanley Coren's study of 79 breeds for intelligence, hounds do not rank highly. Indeed, by this measure, the Afghan Hound, though a fine hunter relying on its sharp vision and great speed, is generally reckoned to be the least intelligent of all domesticated dogs. The most intelligent hound is the Norwegian Elkhound, in 36th place in the Above Average Group.

Improving a hound's intelligence

It is perhaps a side effect of a hound's incredibly acute senses that it is often sidetracked by a passing smell or peripheral activity. So the best way to improve its ability to understand and respond to commands is to improve its concentration. This means keeping on top of its training and continually testing it with "Sit" (see page 103), "Stay" (see page 106), "Come" (see page 105), and "Fetch" (see page 114) commands. Ensure at all times that your dog is fully focused on you with good eye contact. The more you do this, the more its concentration level will improve and the smarter your hound will be.

Pastoral dogs

Some of the cleverest breeds of dog belong to this group. Physically and mentally highly developed and hardy, they work alongside man and can do things no man can do. Few sights are more heartwarming when walking in the countryside than to see a sheepdog gathering a flock of sheep with one eye on his master and ears pricked, awaiting the next whistled command.

Origins

These working dogs are the master tacticians and strategists that have worked alongside shepherds, herdsmen, and farmers for centuries in the marshalling and moving of cloven-footed livestock, such as cattle and sheep and, less commonly, other animals. Some breeds, such as the Portuguese Cattle Dog, were, and in some cases still are, used to work with a variety of stock. Others are also employed for guarding flocks and herds. The beautiful Samoyed originally herded and protected reindeer in its native Siberia and Russian Arctic. The Hungarian Puli herds and drives sheep, and Welsh Corgis were first used as cattle dogs by the ancient Celtic people. The Bearded Collie had almost disappeared by the early part of the 20th century, but the breed was rescued by mating a pair in 1944. The Bouvier des Flanders breed was used as an army dog during World War One where it displayed great strength and courage.

General characteristics

This group comprises a variety of clever, thinking breeds. Physically, pastoral dogs tend to be tough characters, accustomed to hard work in rugged terrain in all weather. Most of them possess a rainproof double coat. Mentally, they are sharp, able to count and calculate, and quick to observe and take action. Pastoral breeds tend to love games involving water, exploration, and hiding objects. Athletic as well as sharp-witted, the Australian Cattle Dog always excels in such dog sports events as Agility, Frisbee, and Flyball competitions.

Individual breeds

Some breeds, such as the Border Collie, simply need to work, and are usually not very happy when kept solely as house pets. Some smaller pastoral types, such as the Lancashire Heeler, do make cheerful companion pets, although they are now rarely used as working animals. The Heeler, once a common

Intelligence	Breed
Brightest Group	Border Collie (1); German Shepherd Dog (3); Shetland Sheepdog (6); Australian Cattle Dog, Welsh Corgi (Pembroke) (10)
Excellent Group	Belgian Tervueren (13); Belgian Sheepdog (15); Belgian Malinois (22); Welsh Corgi (Cardigan) (26)
Above Average Group	Bearded Collie (34)
Average Group	Australian Shepherd Dog (42)
Fair Group	Old English Sheepdog (63)

driver of cattle, running behind the stock and nipping the heels of recalcitrant individuals, still delights in hunting rats. Some years ago I presented a pair to the Windsor Safari Park, in southern England, to control rodents infesting the tiger reserve. They worked at night when the big cats were asleep in their houses and took less than two weeks to eradicate all the rats in the reserve!

Comparative intelligence

It goes without saying that this is a highly intelligent group of breeds, with one of its members, the Border Collie, generally accepted as *the* most intelligent of dogs. Other pastoral dogs come high in the rankings, too, with five placed in the top ten.

Improving a pastoral dog's intelligence

To sharpen up the intelligence of pastoral breeds, concentrate on problem-solving tests and games, such as the Indoor and Outdoor Treasure Hunt and Advanced Treasure Hunt (see pages 87 and 120).

Terriers

These dogs are full of bounce and brightness. Nowadays, they make fascinating, amusing, and loyal pets, and are much more than the underground badger and fox hunters of yesteryear. Most of them are remarkably tough and hardy, but even the Bull terriers, some of which have been sadly transmuted into Pit Bulls and exploited by unsavory characters, have a sunny, gentle disposition in the right hands.

Origins

These breeds were mainly developed in Great Britain. Originally hunting dogs designed for tackling animals such as foxes, badgers, rabbits, and rats underground, terrier types were being used when the Romans first invaded the islands and gave the canine "workers in the earth" the name *terrarii* from the Latin for earth, *terra*. Every corner of Britain produced particular brands of terrier. England brought forth the Fox, Airedale, Bedlington, and Bull, Scotland gave us the Scottish, West Highland, Skye, and Cairn, Wales the Welsh and Sealyham, and Ireland the Irish and Kerry Blue.

General characteristics

Nimble bodies and nimble minds; cocky, resilient, and sparkling, these are the basic characteristics of the terrier group. Nowadays, most terriers make delightful, lively pets and companions. You might expect these spirited, bright, and hardy dogs to be intelligent and indeed they are (see below), but these traits can lead them to be easily distracted, so, once trained, discipline and obedience have to be carefully maintained thereafter by the owner. Otherwise, these perky characters will tend to do as they please when they please. Some "doggy" folk believe terriers are difficult to train because they are simply too smart, independent, sensitive, and, frequently, uncooperative. An opposite opinion is held by professional dog trainers, with whom I often work on films and television commercials. They say the dogs are keen, quick learners that are motivated and sharply focused on the job at hand. Add to that their toughness and ample supplies of energy enabling them to keep working for extended periods of time, and you have some of the best canine performers. Keen outdoor games players, terriers particularly enjoy balls and Frisbees.

Intelligence	Breed
Above Average Group	Airedale Terrier (29); Border Terrier (30); Manchester Terrier (32); Australian Terrier, American Staffordshire Terrier (34); Cairn Terrier, Kerry Blue Terrier (35); Silky Terrier (37); Norwich Terrier (38)
Average Group	Soft-Coated Wheaten Terrier, Bedlington Terrier, Smooth Fox Terrier (40); West Highland White Terrier (47); Staffordshire Bull Terrier (49); Wirehaired Fox Terrier (51); Welsh Terrier, Irish Terrier (53); Boston Terrier (54)
Fair Group	Skye Terrier (55); Norfolk Terrier, Sealyham Terrier (56); Dandie Dinmont Terrier, Tibetan Terrier, Lakeland Terrier (62); Scottish Terrier (65); Bull Terrier (66)

Individual breeds

The most intelligent terrier is the Yorkshire Terrier, although some national Kennel Clubs now assign it to the Toy Group. A diminutive, frequently bedecked and beribboned toy lap dog of great popularity, the Yorkie was developed about 150 years ago and was originally a much bigger animal. Far more than just a decorative pet with long silky hair, the Yorkie is spirited, brave, and self-assured, and makes a good guard dog.

Comparative intellligence

In the list of 79 breeds studied for intelligence by Professor Coren, ten terrier breeds are to be found in the Above Average rankings.

Improving a terrier's intelligence

It is the trainer's control as well as the dog's nature that count in training terriers. Owners can improve their dog's IQ by training in obeying commands (see pages 102–115) and ignoring distractions.

Utility dogs

This is a rather curious name for this group of breeds. The dictionary definition of "utility" is stated as "usefulness or fitness for a purpose." But surely all breeds are therefore utility, for all of them are eminently useful in whatever they are best at doing!

Origins

Among utility dogs are some of the most interesting and unusual kinds dating back to the earliest documented records of breeding. They include the Chow Chow, originally used as a war dog in Mongolia 3,000 years ago, the Poodle, descended from the Pudel, a German game bird retriever that worked in water, the Dalmatian, which trotted alongside horse-drawn carriages in the 19th century to guard the passengers against highwaymen, and the famous Bulldog, once so sadly exploited by man in the barbarities of bull-baiting.

General characerics

This group of dogs, a miscellaneous bunch left over after the other breeds have been neatly pigeonholed, possess "utility"—fitness for a purpose—having been bred for some function not included in the working and sporting categories or purely for aesthetic reasons, with looks pleasing to their owners.

Individual breeds

Four utility breeds, the Shih-Tzu, Lhasa Apso, Miniature Schnauzer, and Dalmatian, were among the 20 most popular dogs in the U.K. in a recent survey, and another four, the Boston Terrier, the Bulldog, the Keeshond, and the Poodle, are the proud national dogs of the U.S., U.K., Holland, and France, respectively.

The Boston Terrier, an intelligent, feisty, bouncy little dog, is one of the few breeds to have been developed in the U.S. and certainly the first non-sporting dog bred there. It originated in the 1870s, when a Mr. Robert Hooper of Boston bought a dog, known as Hooper's Judge, a cross between an English Bulldog and an English White Terrier. Thereafter the breed developed by the introduction of Bull Terrier and French Bulldog blood lines. They were used in the 19th century for the purpose of dog fighting, a "sport" that was centered in Boston. The Boston Terrier Club of America was

Intelligence	Breed
Brightest Group	Poodle (2)
Excellent Group	Miniature Schnauzer (11); Schipperke (14); Keeshond (16); Standard Schnauzer (18)
Above Average Group	Giant Schnauzer (28); Dalmatian (39)
Average Group	Tibetan Spaniel (46); Shar Pei (51); Japanese Akita (54)
Fair Group	French Bulldog (58); Lhasa Apso (68)
Lowest Group	Shih-Tzu (70); Chow Chow (76); Bulldog (77)

eventually recognized in 1891. In the 1960s, a Boston Terrier called Missie was credited with amazing powers of divination, making predictions by moving the hands of a toy clock. It is claimed that in this way she eventually predicted the precise time of her own death!

Comparative intelligence

What about the intelligence of utility dogs? The answer is that it varies from breed to breed as much as their wide range of physical appearance. The Poodle is considered to be the second most intelligent dog, and the Chow Chow and Bulldog among the four least intelligent breeds. Some of them appear in Professor Coren's ranking of intelligence of 79 breeds.

Improving a utility dog's intelligence

The ideal games for utility dogs involve hide and seek (see pages 87 and 120) and exercises requiring thought and skill, such as Professor Coren's tests (see pages 92–95).

Working dogs

After man first domesticated the dog, he began selective breeding to create breeds that were particularly capable of certain types of work in assisting him. The modern Working dog group contains breeds that specialize in a huge range of tasks.

Origins

The variety of skills that the different dog breeds came to master over the millennia of their selective breeding by human beings, derived from the fundamental biological make-up of the dog family, *Canis*, one of the most successful types of mammal on Earth. Intelligence, strength, stamina, speed, excellent sight, a remarkable sense of smell, the sociability of the pack animal, and the natural hunting skills of a predatory carnivore were all there; man had simply to select, concentrate, and exaggerate some of these features by controlled breeding in order to acquire an invaluable, talented assistant in his daily labors.

The working breeds include a renowned rescuer of people in danger of drowning—the Newfoundland and the Bouvier des Flandres, once one of the most skilful cattle dogs in Europe and now used as a guide and tracker, as well as the Alaskan Malamute, a snow lover that has been known to run 100 miles (160 km) in just under 18 hours.

General characteristics

The working dog group comprises a highly colorful variety of specialist breeds. However, common to all working dog breeds is a combination of physical ability and resourcefulness that displays what can be termed "the canine work ethic."

Individual breeds

The Alaskan Malamute is one of the greatest characters among the working breeds, descended from the dogs living with the Mahlemuit Inuit tribe of western Alaska. This tough and resourceful sled dog accompanied the miners who came to Alaska in the Gold Rush of 1896 and, later, Admiral Richard Byrd on his expedition to the South Pole in 1928–30. Highly intelligent but easily bored, the Malamute can be tricky to train and prone to becoming involved in mischief, particularly digging. It is very friendly, perhaps excessively so, toward people and, consequently, does not make much of a guard dog. With other dogs, its dominating nature tends to lead to aggression, and it is frequently predatorily

Intelligence	Breed
Brightest Group	Dobermann Pinscher (5); Rottweiler (9)
Excellent Group	Bernese Mountain Dog (22)
Above Average Group	Bouvier des Flandres (29); Newfoundland (34)
Average Group	Siberian Husky (45); Boxer, Great Dane (48); Alaskan Malamute (50)
Fair Group	St. Bernard (65)
Lowest Group	Mastiff (72)

inclined toward smaller animals. Malamutes do sometimes bark, but in general they tend to vocalize by making a "woo, woo" or "murr, murr" sound. When lonely or unhappy, they may howl in the manner of wolves.

Comparative intelligence

In judging the intelligence of the different working breeds, it is crucial and indeed only fair to consider their IQ in relation to what they were bred to do, their brainpower being focused on one particular field of activity. The intelligence of a desert-working sight hound is clearly different from that of a foxhunter's terrier or a snow specialist draught breed. As you might expect with such a varied bunch, their ranking on the Coren intelligence table is widely spread.

Improving a working dog's intelligence

The intelligence of these dogs can be enhanced by involving them in games that enable them to utilize the natural physical and mental abilities of their breed, whether it be action in the form of, say, visual skills, or thought, as in problem solving. It is best not to play rougher games such as "tug o' war" or wrestling with them, however, as their dominant nature may release tendencies for aggression.

Toy dogs

These breeds may be ornamental, but, nevertheless, they serve mankind in ways that are equally important as those of the working, pastoral, and utility dogs. Many of them make excellent guard dogs, quick to alert their owners to intruders.

Origins

Since 1863, the word "toy" as applied to dogs has simply meant "diminutive." The majority of toy breeds were originally bred for their decorative appearance. It is written that, when the Chinese Empress entered her palace in the Forbidden City, 100 Japanese Chins would stand up on their hind legs until she took her seat. A few toy breeds, however, were working dogs at one time.

General characteristics

This is a group that specializes as much as any of the others, in their case in being aesthetically pleasing, companion animals. Their ability is not just limited to "looking cute;" they play an important role in the lives of those who live alone, the elderly, the sick, and the housebound. It has been proved that they are therapeutic in improving the well-being of such folk, and are increasingly taken to hospital patients to assist in boosting morale and thereby shortening convalescence. In addition, their strong sense of loyalty and family often makes

them excellent guard dogs, warning of the presence of strangers with barks and yelps, and if they think it appropriate, actually attacking intruders.

Individual breeds

So-called Turnspits were toy dogs that were in use until the middle of the 19th century in the great households of England and America to save cooks the effort of turning meat on a spit by hand. The Turnspit was placed in a small wheel that was connected to the spit. As the dog ran, the meat would be turned. In order to avoid a dog becoming exhausted with its work, they were often kept in pairs, turning the wheel alternately. Many people believe that the now-extinct Turnspit was related to the Glen of Imaal Terrier, in modern times a member of the terrier group.

In medieval times, people often took dogs with them to church to use as "foot warmers." During a service in Bath Abbey, England, where there was a sprinkling of dogs among the congregation, the first

Intelligence	Breed
Brightest Group	Papillon (8)
Excellent Group	Pomeranian (23)
Above Average Group	Yorkshire Terrier (27); Affenpinscher, Miniature Pinscher (37)
Average Group	Cavalier King Charles Spaniel (44); Bichon Frise, English Toy Spaniel (45)
Fair Group	Brussels Griffon, Maltese (59); Japanese Chin (62); Chihuahua (67)
Lowest Group	Pekingese (73)

lesson included verses from the Book of Ezekiel that referred to "wheels" and "the animals that control them." On hearing these words, the bright little dogs, according to a witness "...all clapt their Tails between their Legs and ran out of Church!"

Comparative intelligence

As with other groups, toy breeds vary in their level of intelligence. Do not be deceived into thinking that their looks and small size mean that they are in any way birdbrained. Size has nothing to do with

intelligence, and some toys score very highly in intelligence tests. According to Professor Coren's ranking, the Papillon is one of the brightest dogs, although the Pekingese is relegated to the lowest degree of working/obedience intelligence.

Improving a toy dog's intelligence

The intelligence of these small animals, which are far more than mere ornaments, can be developed significantly by games and tests of thought and skill (see pages 87, 115, and 130).

Sporting dogs (Gundogs)

These popular dogs are not nowadays to be found mainly accompanying hunters but in family homes. Bright, loving, and loyal, breeds such as the retrievers and spaniels are among the most popular, particularly where there are children.

Origins

These dogs come in a wide variety of breeds, all of which were developed to act as hunters' assistants in some fashion, mainly by finding and retrieving game. They hunt principally by picking up scents carried in the air. To do this kind of work, a dog has to be sharp, focused, and highly obedient.

Characteristics of the different types

The wide variety of breeds in the group are divided into three sections:

Spaniels

These are medium-sized dogs that stand not too high off the ground. They have a well-developed muzzle, a keen nose, and ears that are protected by long flaps—all very sensible features for animals that must work in rough countryside. Some breeds can hunt and retrieve, others retrieve only, with most of them ranging over the ground ahead of the hunter but still staying relatively close to the gun.

Retrievers

Retrievers are hunting specialists. Strong and well-built, they are expert "finders and returners" of game, often after the latter have been flushed by spaniels.

Pointers and setters

These are generally bigger than spaniels and with longer legs. These dogs move far ahead of the hunter and, when they scent game, do not immediately disturb the birds into flying, but stand rigidly with muzzle stretched toward the quarry ("point") or drop to the ground ("set").

Individual breeds

Many dog lovers are puzzled by the meaning of the word "tolling" in the name of the Canadian breed of gundog, the Nova Scotia Duck-Tolling Retriever. This fine animal, looking rather like a small Golden Retriever, tolls (lures) wild ducks to within range of the guns by playing a game of "fetch the stick" with the hunter. A stick is thrown into the water several times and is quickly retrieved by the dog. "Tollers" can happily play the game for hours! The activity of

Intelligence	Breed
Brightest Group	Golden Retriever (4); Labrador Retriever (7)
Excellent Group	English Springer Spaniel (12); German Shorthaired Pointer (17); Flat-Coated Retriever, English Cocker Spaniel (18); Brittany (19); Cocker Spaniel (20); Weimaraner (21); Irish Water Spaniel (24)
Above Average Group	Chesapeake Bay Retriever (27); Welsh Springer Spaniel (31); Field Spaniel (34); Irish Setter (35); English Setter, Clumber Spaniel (37)
Average Group	Pointer (43); German Wirehaired Pointer (44)

the dog attracts the curiosity of the birds, which paddle toward their nemesis to take a closer look. As soon as they are within range, the hunter fires and the dog retrieves the fallen game.

Originating in Nova Scotia in the 19th century from so-called Red Decoy dogs brought from England, Tollers carry retriever and working spaniel blood in their veins. The breed is very popular in North America and there are many Toller breed clubs in the U.S., where it is known as an intelligent, playful, and patient animal, a superb companion and family dog that gets along well with children and other pets.

Comparative intelligence

All of these breeds are very intelligent, with two of them appearing in the top ten of Professor Coren's Brightest Group and eight in the Excellent Working Group. None of them fall into the Fair or Lowest Groups in these intelligence rankings.

Improving a gundog's intelligence

As one might expect, the intelligence of these dogs is best promoted by tests and games dependent on their innate physical abilities and which involve searching and tracking, in some breeds by sight and in others by scent (see pages 87, 120, and 130).

Mongrels

If you are looking for a canine pet and aren't aiming for a particular pedigree, mongrels, with the hardiness that their possession of so-called hybrid vigor gives them, are just right for you. Rescue centers and dogs' homes can show you any number of crossbred dogs in all sizes, shapes, colors, and patterns. They may not display the finer points of conformation that delight show bench judges, but they all possess abundant character—far more important than physical perfection.

Origins

You could argue that almost all pedigree dogs are mongrels, in that they were originally produced by mating together different kinds of dog. Some of the most recent examples are the Labradoodle, the Black Russian Terrier (a product of some 20 different breeds developed by Russian Red Army scientists during World War II), and a range of Wolfdogs. All domestic dogs belong to the species *Canis familiaris*. Most mongrels are the result of natural rather than artificial selection, and with the Darwinian principle of survival of the fittest playing a crucial part by ensuring that the hardiest, healthiest, happiest animals survive, "good" genetic material tends to become dominant and passed down by them. This so-called "hybrid vigor" also tends to make them better tempered and more adaptable than pedigree types.

Pedigree breeds, fancy as they now may be, are all, through artificial selective breeding by man over the centuries, descended originally from mongrels. Like humans, whose lineages have passed through countless races and nationalities, there is strictly no such thing as a pure bred canine individual. The new crossbreeds of today, the Labradoodles and such, will eventually progress to the status of "pedigree" as far as future kennel clubs are concerned. For now, however, they are mongrels, mixed breeds, mutts or, as they are called in the U.S. when involved in competitive sports, All American dogs. Good for all of them!

General characteristics

Mongrels are at least as rich in desirable qualities as the most aristocratic of "posh" pedigree dogs. Obviously the mongrel will display some of the behavioral as well as the physical features of its pedigree forebears. If you know or can guess the breeds that contributed to a particular mongrel, its character may be the sum of any one of a number of possible combinations of its pedigree forebears'

Mongrel type	Characteristics
Sheepdog/Collie-type crossbreed	These dogs display the sharp intelligence and loyalty of their pedigree relatives and, like them, need plenty of outdoor exercise. Great companions, but not lap dogs.
Toy-type crossbreed	Affectionate, loyal, and excellent guard dogs, they make superb lap-dog-type companions for older folk and are happy living in town and city dwellings.
Small terrier-type crossbreed	Multipurpose pets happy in town or country. Intelligent, active, lively, and loyal, they also make superb guard dogs.
Retriever-type crossbreed	Family favorites, these dogs are loving, gentle, and affectionate with children. They require plenty of regular outdoor exercise and are thus better suited to country than city life.
German Shepherd Dog-type crossbreed	These popular dogs are loyal and highly intelligent. They make first-rate house guards, but as they need lots of vigorous exercise, they are not suitable for a city dwelling.

various qualities, some appearing as dominant, others as recessive in its make up. Some Labradoodles, for example, will be mentally much more retriever than Poodle, while others will be the reverse, or roughly 50:50.

What would the typical mongrel look like if all the dogs in the world were turned loose to interbreed? Essentially, it would be a happy medium of a dog with no extremes of physical form or function. The body would be shapely and well defined with a moderate, not overstretched, back and a muscular neck of good length. The head would have good bone structure with a fairly well-developed nose, pert and expressive ears, and bright eyes with an alert, lively expression. The coat would be neither too short nor too long, the legs strong and well proportioned, and the tail of medium length. The size overall could be small, medium, or large.

Main types
Most pet dogs worldwide are mongrels, and if you are looking for a good companion, there is no better place to go than your local humane societies and shelters.

The Wolfdog hybrid
A Wolfdog is not a mongrel (a cross between one or more breeds of a single species) but a hybrid (a cross between animals of different species) that has gained some popularity in recent years. There are thought to be around 300,000 of them in the U.S. Several states require a license to keep hybrids, a few states prohibit them, and many states do not regulate them at all. This controversial cross between wolf (*Canis lupus*) and one or more of a variety of domestic dog breeds (*Canis familiaris*) is considered dangerous by many dog experts and must be licensed under the Dangerous Wild Animals Act legislation in the U.K.

Because they retain much of the wolf's predatory instinct, a high percentage of attacks by them have involved small children, considered by the animal at the time as prey animals. It should, however, be emphasized that predatory behavior, at which wolves excel, is *not* the same as aggression. Many Wolfdog owners state that, on the contrary, they are gentle, good-natured creatures. Certainly, the wolf in the wild tends to be less aggressive within its society than domestic dogs are, and the most difficult and risky Wolfdog hybrids are those where their aggressive nature comes from carrying genes inherited from breeds of dog such as Rottweilers or Dobermanns, not from wolves. But other definitely undesirable characteristics of the Wolfdog are derived from its lupine half—for example, destructiveness and a great urge to dig and keep digging. They are skilled and determined escape artists. Therefore, Wolfdogs are not to be recommended as pets for most people.

Comparative intelligence
Hybrid vigor (see page 78) ensures that mongrels tend to be at least as intelligent as their pedigree relations; some dog owners would claim more so. The reason may be the fact that mongrels on average possess bigger brains than pedigrees, either as a result of genetic expression of hybrid vigor or because the more interesting experiences a dog has from puppyhood onward, somewhat more likely in down-to-earth crossbreeds than pampered show-bench specimens, the bigger the brain is stimulated to grow.

Improving a mongrel's intelligence
As mongrels come in all shapes and sizes, owners should play games with and set tasks for their dogs that draw upon the innate characteristics of the breeds that make them up—problem solving if they are carrying pastoral or gundog blood (see pages 94–95), obedience to a range of commands if terrier types (see pages 102–111), and reinforcing their ability to concentrate during training if some of their forebears seem likely to have been hounds. But for all mongrels, whatever the "mix," as indeed for all pedigree pets, training to respond quickly and reliably to voice or visual commands is essential and should be constantly maintained.

How **intelligent** is your dog?

This is not an easy question to answer, and one that requires considerable, fascinating and entertaining testing of the animal on the part of you, the owner. No one test alone can rate a dog's intelligence, and some tests are more appropriate for certain breeds. The lifestyle of a dog is, to a large extent, reflected in its "intelligence" as perceived by people. On the one hand, we have the Border Collie out working at a range of tasks in all weather, and, on the other, the Pekingese that needs to do little except agree to be pampered in comfortable surroundings.

As with people, dogs of the same age and type vary immensely in intelligence. The Coren league tables of canine intelligence (see page 18) tell only a part, and a contentious part at that, of the story. It is not realistic simply to look up your pet's position in the tables and then inform the world that your beloved "Fido" is 25 rungs higher up the IQ ladder than your neighbor's "Towser." Each dog is an individual with its own personal genetic history and experience of life. Problem-solving tests depend not only on a dog's intellectual powers, but also on his physical make up and the behavioral characteristics of his breed.

Experiments in canine **intelligence**

Intelligence tests for children have a controversial history. For dogs, intelligence tests have similarly given rise to debate among scientists as to how to go about estimating and comparing IQ levels with any degree of accuracy.

Tracking test

An experiment required Beagles and Bloodhounds to follow the trail of a man going through woodland. After walking a little while, the "quarry" stepped up onto the fallen trunk of a tree and continued along it for several feet. The Beagles all lost the scent at the point where the man left the ground. The Bloodhounds also lost the scent at the same place, but only for a second or two, after which they lifted their heads and found it again. This does not prove that Bloodhounds are more intelligent than Beagles, but merely that the latter have shorter legs! Tests of this kind cannot be used to measure intelligence.

Maze-solving tests

Another test that researchers have used with several breeds, including Cocker Spaniels, Beagles, Basenjis, Fox Terriers, and Shelties, examined their ability to find their way out of a maze. At first, the Fox Terriers and Shelties did rather badly, while the Beagles and Basenjis excelled at it. However, it is wrong to conclude that the two latter breeds are mentally brighter than the others. Rather, the Beagles' aptitude was due to their quick exploratory movements, a trait of a breed developed to hunt small game, while the Basenjis were good for a different reason—their keen vision enabled them to pick up visual clues leading to a solution. Continuing with the tests, it was found that the Terriers and Shelties improved their performance, while that of the Beagles worsened! The reason seems to be that Terriers and Shelties are very good at learning repetitive behaviors, whereas Beagles, whose inquisitive nature makes their behavior variable, do not perform well in repetition.

Doing your own testing

There are a number of simple tests that can easily be applied to the family dog in order to make a light-hearted assessment of your pet's intelligence.

Put your dog to the **test**

If you want to try rating your pet's IQ, I have drawn up a range of easily performed tests together with a scoring system. You should repeat the tests again in the future to see if your dog gets the same score. The results might improve dramatically, particularly if you follow my advice on training's role in improving intelligence (see Making your dog smarter, pages 96–117).

The nature of the tests

The following pages present a number of tests and games designed to challenge your pet's intelligence by determining his ability and speed in solving problems, as well as his powers of memory, observation, and comprehension. They also involve linking known verbal commands (see pages 102–113) to some new forms of nonverbal cue.

Pre-requisites

All tests work best where there is a close relationship between dog and owner, with both parties interacting with one another regularly and often, and particularly so if the animal is obedience trained to a reasonable degree. The dog should be over one year of age, have known his owner for at least six months, and lived in the home where the tests are carried out for at least two to three months.

Scoring

There are scoring methods for some of the tests, but bear in mind that certain tests are more appropriate to some breeds rather than others because of the animals' inbred physical and/or behavioral characteristics. Intelligence tests are invaluable as improvers and developers of canine intelligence. Challenge your dog with them regularly by treating them more as games than tests, and you will find that gradually your pet's score will rise.

Packet puzzler

This is a simply executed problem-solving test for your dog. Any breed of dog should be able to tackle it, though snub-nosed characters tend not to do as well as those with longer snouts.

Method
Put a treat in a square of stiff paper and fold it twice to enclose it. Put the packet down in front of the dog.

How does your dog rate?
Bright problem solvers will use only their paws to open the packet.
Average problem solvers will use their mouth and paws.
The rest will not open the packet and simply play with it.

Peek-a-boo barrier

Again, this test explores the dog's ability to analyze a situation and then take appropriate, efficient action—the core of animal intelligence. The Pastoral group of dogs excels at this test, as you might expect.

Method
Make a barrier from cardboard that is 5 ft (1.5 m) wide and higher than the dog when it stands up on its hind legs. Cut a 3 in (7.5 cm) wide vertical slot in the center running from 4 in (10 cm) from the top to 4 in (10 cm) from the bottom. Support the barrier so that it stands firmly using blocks or boxes. With you on one side of the barrier and the dog on the other, show your pet a treat.

How does your dog rate?
Bright dogs will move around the barrier to claim the treat in under 30 seconds.
Fairly bright dogs will take 30–60 seconds.
Not very bright dogs will shove their heads in the aperture and get stuck or keep pushing.

Variation
Have the dog on the other side of a fence or wall from you, but through which, via a gap, window, or hole, he can see you. The only way he can get to you when you call is by running away from you and around the end of the barrier.

How does your dog rate?
Bright dogs immediately run around the end of the barrier and come to you, jump over the barrier or try to jump over, fail and then run around the end of the barrier.
Not very bright dogs try to jump over the barrier, fail, but then just sit there.
Dimmer dogs (but still adorable) don't do anything but sit and perhaps yelp.

Outdoor treasure hunt

This game tests general intelligence and tracking powers. Toy dogs tend not to do so well in this test as compared with the Indoor treasure hunt. The test is best done when there are no other dogs in the vicinity.

1 On a walk with your dog, hide some treats—for instance, in a clump of grass or behind a tree—in full view of him, but do not permit him to start searching until you give permission. Make things more difficult by hiding the treats on fences or low branches of bushes.

2 Instead of food treats, use your dog's favorite toy. Tell the dog to "Sit-Stay" (see pages 103 and 106), then walk off, dropping the toy at some point onto one of your footprints. Walk back to the dog by a different route and then send him off to search. He will follow the scent of your shoes and, hopefully, come upon the toy and retrieve it.

Indoor treasure hunt

This game is more of a memory rather than an intelligence test, although generally "brighter" individuals do better at it. Easy to do, it is fun for both owner and pet. This test is best for small and medium-sized dogs.

1 Go around your home, accompanied by your pet so that he can see what you are doing, hiding edible treats in a variety of places, all within reach yet not easy to see, such as behind a sofa, beneath a bed, under a cushion, and so on. The treats should be dog or ordinary biscuits. When hiding the treats, be sure to walk all over the floor in each room, not simply straight to the chosen hiding place. This stops the dog finding the treats by merely tracking your footsteps.

2 Now take your pet into a room where nothing has been hidden. After half a minute, release the dog and let him search the home. Follow him in silence and see how many treats he can find and how quickly. This tests short-term memory. To test long-term memory, repeat, but wait ten minutes before letting the dog go searching.

Mental maneuvers

These three simple tests can be done if your pet is trained to perform a routine behavior, such as Sit (see page 103). They examine the dog's ability to link different nonverbal cues to what is required of him.

Method 1
Clap your hands and then say "Sit,"or whichever other command you have chosen to use. Repeat ten times. Now clap your hands without giving the "Sit" command. If your dog sits down, he has learned that a clap means the same as "Sit," If he does not sit down, repeat the procedure of clap followed by "Sit" another ten times, then try the clap alone once more.

Method 2
Hold your clenched fist in front of the dog's face. Open and close your hand quickly and then say "Sit." How many repetitions does it take for it to obey the signal without it being accompanied by a verbal command?

Method 3
Dip a cotton wool bud in something with a distinct aroma, such as toothpaste or rosewater. Hold in front of the dog's nose and give the verbal command. After several repetitions with the dog performing the behavior correctly, substitute a clean, unmoistened bud. If the dog performs the behavior (by using the bud as a *visual* cue), walk away and ignore him for half a minute, then repeat the test. Rate your dog as before.

How does your dog rate?
For each method:
Very bright dogs make the mental link after only 10 repetitions.
Bright dogs learn after 10–50 repetitions.
Dimmer dogs still don't get it after 50 repetitions, so try something else—your hands will be sore from clapping!

Advanced training
If your dog understands quickly, go on to use a variety of sound, visual, and scent cues for different behaviors. You may be able to reach the point, for example, where your pet will sit when presented with the odor of vanilla essence and lie down when you let it smell cheese!

Find the treat

This test is essentially that used by Hungarian researchers (see page 12). It tests memory and is generally a useful measure of intelligence. You will need five or six identical containers, such as tins or nontransparent jars, with tight-fitting, preferably screw-on tops.

1 Open one container in full view of your pet and put inside a favorite treat of some sort after showing it to the dog. Replace the top firmly. Now "shuffle" all the containers around on the floor, keeping your eye on the treat-filled one.

2 Now the dog has to find the correct container, helped only by a signal from you, and to be successful, this must be his *first* choice. Point at the tin or jar when starting the test and say nothing. If your pet gets it right, open the container and give the treat, together with plenty of praise. If his initial choice is the wrong one, repeat the whole procedure again from the beginning.

> **How does your dog rate?**
> **Very bright dogs** learn in less than 4 repetitions.
> **Bright dogs** learn after 4–10 repetitions.
> **Average dogs** take more than 10 repetitions.

Advanced training

Later, once your dog has mastered your pointing signal, you can try indicating by some other means, such as nodding at or even just looking steadily at the container.

Rico's memory test

Is your dog another Rico (see page 60), able to accumulate a vocabulary of many dozens of words? All dogs have a well-developed memory bank in which they can store words uttered by humans.

1 Take two different objects, say, plastic toys. Throw one and say "Fetch the..." When the dog retrieves it and brings it back to you, give fulsome praise and a treat. Repeat over and over again with the same object until he is quick and reliable in response.

2 Now do the same test with the second object until prompt retrieval has been mastered by the dog.

3 Throw both toys together and ask the dog for one. Give praise when the correct item is retrieved. Increase the number of objects.

> **How does your dog rate?**
> **Very bright dogs** may learn 60 words.
> **Bright dogs** may learn 30 words.
> **Average dogs** may learn 15 words.

Spot the difference

These are quite simple tests of observational powers and memory. The first is dependent upon your pet being familiar with the time of day when you take him out for a walk and the preparations that herald the event, such as putting on your coat and getting the lead.

Method 1
At a time of day when you do *not* usually go for a walk, go through the usual preparations, but do not call the dog or go to the door.

Method 2
When the dog is out, rearrange some of the furniture in a room with which he is familiar—add a chair or a big sofa cushion, alter the position of a table, and so on.

> **How does your dog rate?**
> **Method 1**
> **Very bright dogs** will bring their lead to you!
> **Bright dogs** will immediately either run happily to the door or to you.
>
> **Method 2**
> **Bright dogs** will, when they next come into the room, immediately notice that things have changed and begin exploring and sniffing.

Canine accountancy

This is a test of basic intelligence. You will need a number of more or less identical objects, such as colored balls, a piece of board to act as a screen, and a stopwatch. Ideally, the dog should be familiar with the balls, but in any case, let him inspect and, if possible, play with them before beginning the test.

1 Sit on the floor with the dog about 6½ ft (2 m) away from you. Place the screen between you, supported by a brick or other weight. Show the dog one ball *above* the screen, then lower it behind your side of the screen and place on the floor, then gradually progress until seven balls are initially shown to the dog. Surreptitiously remove or add a ball or balls to them or leave the number unchanged, unseen by the dog.

2 Take away the screen so that the dog can see the group of balls, starting the stopwatch at the same moment. Look at the dog's eyes. Is it staring at the balls? If so, time the duration of his gaze. Repeat, changing or retaining the number of balls as you decide. Measure the time the dog stares at the group of balls on each occasion.

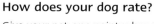

How does your dog rate?

Give your pet one point when its lengthened gaze time indicates it has spotted something amiss and double points if it does so when more than four balls are involved. The total number of points obtained after 20 "challenges" can be used as a rough indication of one aspect of the dog's intelligence.

Very bright dogs will score over 14 points.
Bright dogs will score 10–14 points.
Average dogs will score 5–10 points.

If your pet consistently fails to pay attention or seems not to be aware of your skulduggery at all, you can assume that his talents lie in fields other than canine accountancy!

Test your **dog's IQ**

Professor Coren's book *The Intelligence of Dogs* (see page 18) contains a large number of tests that he has devised for testing canine intelligence. Some of them, together with their scoring systems, are described below. Apply all the tests and then add all the scores. The total score gives a rough guide to your pet's IQ.

Language comprehension

The dog should be settled around 6½ ft (2 m) in front of you. In the normal tone of voice you use when calling your dog, call "Refrigerator" (the choice of word is not important). The dog is not expected to think he *is*, all of a sudden, a refrigerator, but simply to realize that you are addressing him using a word that is new to him and that *you are talking to him*.

Scoring
- If the dog shows some response, score 3 points.
- If the dog does not come, call "Television" in the same tone.
- If the dog comes, score 2 points.
- If the dog still has not responded, call his name.
- If the dog comes or shows any tendency to move toward you, score 5 points.
- If the dog still has not moved, call his name a second time.
- If the dog comes, score 4 points.
- If the dog still does not come, score 1 point.

Food under can

For this food-finding variation you will need an empty can, such as a soup can, but without any sharp edges, or a similar nontransparent container, a desirable food titbit, and a stopwatch.

1 Command your dog to "Sit–Stay" (see pages 103 and 106) or, if he will not stay, get someone to hold him by his collar. Show your dog the tidbit and let him sniff it.

2 With the dog's full attention, slowly place the food on the ground about 6½ ft (2 m) away. While the dog continues to watch, invert the can over it. Start timing and verbally encourage your pet to get the food.

Scoring
- If the dog retrieves the food in less than 5 seconds, score 5 points.
- If he takes 5–15 seconds, score 4 points.
- If he takes 15–30 seconds, score 3 points.
- If he takes 30–60 seconds, score 2 points.
- If the dog sniffs around the can but does not get the titbit within 60 seconds, score 1 point.

Food under towel

For this food-retrieval test you will need a hand towel, a substantial piece of one of your dog's favorite tidbits, such as a dog biscuit, and a stopwatch.

1 Command your dog to "Sit-Stay" (see pages 103 and 106) or, if he will not stay, get someone to hold him by his collar. Show your dog the titbit and let him sniff it.

2 Slowly place the food on the ground about 6½ ft (2 m) away. While the dog continues to watch, cover the food with the towel.

3 Start timing and verbally encourage your pet to get the food.

Scoring

- If the dog retrieves the food in less than 15 seconds, score 5 points.
- If he takes 15–30 seconds, score 4 points.
- If he takes 30–60 seconds, score 3 points.
- If the dog tries to get the food but gives up, score 2 points.
- If he doesn't even try, score 1 point.

Canine Houdini

This test involves the liberty-loving dog analyzing his suddenly imposed situation and then quickly taking physical action to return it to normality. You will need a large bath towel and a stopwatch.

1 With the dog awake and reasonably active, let him sniff the towel so he gets used to the sight and smell of it.

2 With a quick, smooth motion, throw the towel over the dog so that his head and shoulders are completely covered. Start timing but remain silent.

Scoring

Time how long it takes for the dog to free himself, awarding points as follows:

- In less than 5 seconds, score 5 points.
- In 5–15 seconds, score 4 points
- In 15–30 seconds, score 3 points
- In 30–60 seconds, score 2 points.
- If he has not freed himself after 60 seconds, score 1 point.

Smiling test

This involves a key characteristic of the dog, one that has been so vitally important to domestication—its ability to interact with, understand, and "read" the human being.

1 Have your dog sitting about 6½ ft (2 m) away from you. You must not have told it to sit or stay. Simply pick the right time.

2 Stare intently at the dog's face. When your pet looks at you, count silently to three seconds and then smile broadly.

Scoring

- If he comes to you with tail wagging, score 5 points.
- If he comes slowly or only part of the way with no tail wag, score 4 points.
- If he stands or rises to a sit, but doesn't move toward you, score 3 points.
- If he moves away from you, score 2 points.
- If he pays no attention, score 1 point.

Problem solving and manipulation

This test displays the dog's ability to combine his thinking powers with appropriate action to a particular end. You will need a low table, a substantial piece of a favorite food, and a stopwatch.

1 Make sure the dog is watching you and you have his concentration. Show him the titbit and let him sniff it.

2 With the dog's full attention, slowly place the titbit under the table where your pet can reach with his paw to retrieve it.

3 Start timing and verbally encourage him to get the food.

Scoring

- If he uses his paws to get the food in less than 60 seconds, score 5 points.
- If he takes 1–3 minutes, score 4 points.
- If he uses his muzzle only but has not retrieved after 3 minutes, score 3 points.
- If he simply sniffs and gives one or two tries with his muzzle, score 2 points.
- If no attempt is made to retrieve after 3 minutes, score 1 point.

Cup and treat

This is a slightly different version of the food-retrieval test on page 93. In my experience, terriers and Pastoral dogs perform the best.

1 Place a treat under one of two inverted cups while someone else restrains the dog. Be sure that the dog sees you doing it.

2 Take the dog out of the room for 15 minutes. To eliminate the possibility that the dog uses its sense of smell to locate the treat, put a treat under the *other* cup as well.

3 Bring him back into the room and see if he goes straight for the cup under which you placed the original treat.

Scoring

- If the dog goes straight to the correct cup, knocks it over and takes the treat, score 4 points.
- If the dog goes straight to the correct cup, but takes more than 15 seconds before knocking it over and taking the treat, score 3 points.
- If the dog goes to the correct cup but does not knock it over in under a minute, score 2 points.
- If the dog goes to the wrong cup and knocks it over or does not pay much attention to either cup, score 0 points.

How does your dog rate?

Now add up your pet's total score for the seven tests.

Caneinsteins score over 30 points!

Very bright dogs score 25–30 points.

Not too bright to average dogs score 15–25 points.

If your dog scores less than 15 points, who cares—you adore him anyway!

Making your dog **smarter**

There are three separate components in canine intelligence: the adaptive, the working or obedience, and the instinctive. All dogs, pedigree or mongrel, dullard or clearly brilliant, possess a mixture of the three. Instinctive intelligence is genetic, and consists of inherited abilities and predispositions. There is nothing an owner can do to modify intelligence of this type. However, things can be done to improve the adaptive and working forms of intelligence.

With all dogs, particularly terriers and hounds, which are easily distracted, the most important area to concentrate on is obedience—training, reinforcing, and then continually maintaining the dog's quick responses to commands and the correct performance of the essential behaviors that are the foundations of adaptive and working intelligence—watch, sit, down, come, stay, and so on.

The basic principles are: start as early in life as possible, keep the dog's mind and body active, and give a good, balanced diet throughout his life. Give your dog plenty to think about both when at home and out for exercise. Change his toys regularly, play a variety of games with him, and vary the routes of your daily walks, introducing new places, objects, and people. Most importantly, train your dog in the basic behaviors. Progress from there to train other tricks that enhance obedience and play games that encourage problem solving.

Training to improve intelligence

In both humans and dogs, intelligence is not something an individual is born with and then remains static at a certain level throughout life. It can be improved. Innate "natural" intelligence can be expanded by education. As more and more information is received and stored in the brain cells, the animals "wisdom," its intelligence, will increase. For dogs, training methods are the best way of raising your pet's IQ—maybe even to genius level.

The benefits

Training a dog in basic obedience and more advanced behaviors is fun for both animal and owner. Apart from providing mental and physical exercise, it tightens the bond between pet and owner, and sharpens the dog's intelligence. That latter phrase may not be strictly correct in many cases; an untrained dog may be genetically highly intelligent but has never had the opportunity to demonstrate his talents, and the training regime merely reveals the intelligence lying within the animal. If training is fun and interesting, and brings rewards, the dog is motivated to do well.

The importance of communication

Often when owners think a dog is lacking in intelligence, it is because he is simply viewing the world around him differently, and the human being is not communicating very well. Some pets cope better with poorly communicating owners than others, but we should always endeavor to bridge the communication gap and enhance the relationship.

To communicate with the dog, we have two forms of language—body language and words. As explained earlier (see pages 51–55), body language is crucial in canine understanding of its environment. Dogs can spot minute changes and nuances of posture, gesture, and expression. You must be consistent at all times in the body movements you use when interacting with your pet, just as you use the same words when giving verbal instructions. He will then learn to understand these movements and

"read" your signals. With old dogs that become deaf, the body language of the owner becomes doubly important in maintaining effective communication.

Use of vocabulary

Although dogs cannot speak, they can learn the meaning of our words, sometimes accumulating quite an extensive vocabulary—as with children, so with dogs. Talking to them regularly adds to their vocabulary and develops their intelligence. Once they know the meaning of a number of words, you can go on to string a number together to form a command sentence. A dog trained to **"fetch"** that also knows the meaning of **"slipper"** and the identity of **"Granddad"** can easily be told to **"Fetch the slipper for Granddad."**

When training your dog, in the same way as you need to be consistent in your body language, so you must be with the words you use. Always use the same word for any particular behavior. When you mean "Stop," don't confuse the animal by using colloquial alternatives like "No, you don't!"

Use of sound quality

The sound of your voice in training or indeed whenever you are communicating with your dog should be cheerful and smooth, never loud or harsh, but always consistent in pitch, tone, and volume for any particular command. Learn which pitch and tone of voice works best for each behavior during training. Use praise abundantly during play periods, so that the dog will come to value praise in itself as a reward during training sessions.

Link your body language to the words you use by, for example, demonstrating to the dog what "Sit" means by sitting down in a relaxed pose beside him on different occasions and locations. Stroking the dog slowly when using a word like "Sit" in a warm and gentle tone of voice will link the quality of the sound and the touch to the command on future occasions. Your pet will come to understand that calm speech signifies a calm ambience. A scary voice may frighten the animal into doing the opposite of what is required, and an agitated voice can make dogs become excited and lose control. Never shout. With their acute sense of hearing, dogs listen to you more intently when you speak softly.

The **principles** of training

Training a dog can be done well or badly. It takes time and patience but the rewards for both pet and owner can be enormous. Some people prefer to go to dog training classes or engage a professional dog trainer, but for most owners the methods I outline here are interesting, easy, and productive of remarkable results.

Reinforcing correct behavior

Training by reward with a treat in the form of a scrap of food, a pat of the head, a play together, or praise given when the dog behaves correctly is known as "positive reinforcement." "Negative reinforcement" is a check or punishment that the dog dislikes and withdrawing it when the correct behavior is performed. It is normally used in conjunction with "positive reinforcement," A third form of reinforcement, "secondary reinforcement" is also often used nowadays in dog training. It is particularly useful where it is not appropriate or possible to reward a correctly performed behavior at the proper time. The commonest form of "secondary reinforcer" is a small handheld clicker. The click tells the dog that he has performed correctly and that a reward will be forthcoming.

Punishment

This should only be used in dog training with the greatest circumspection. Force is not a good training tool. Hitting a dog teaches him to stay out of range, whereas training depends on close contact and a good relationship. There are times when you might have to punish a dog to stop him from doing something or to gain his attention. Think carefully why you are using the punishment and be sure that the dog will understand why he is being punished. There is no point in scolding the dog for something he did some time earlier; retribution must be speedy, otherwise it is just counterproductive.

No kind of corporal punishment must *ever* be used on a dog. Hitting, beating, kicking, pressing the lips down hard on the teeth—all of these are utterly taboo. Acceptable punishments are to interrupt whatever the dog is doing in a strong, sharp, even startling way, perhaps by the use of an air horn, the rattle of a can, a puff from a citronella aerosol, a squirt of water, or just a firm, scolding "No!"

Another reasonable punishment is to grasp the skin at the back of the neck (with large dogs, use both hands on either side of the neck) and raise the dog just off the ground—this is how a bitch would naturally punish a puppy. Give him a gentle shake and a verbal scolding at the same time. A simpler measure, a light slap on the rump, will often suffice.

Whenever an undesirable behavior has been interrupted and punished, make a point of going on to encourage a display of good behavior, with rewards if all goes well. Always accompany punishment and reward with verbal signals like "Bad dog" and "Good dog." Later, these will be sufficient punishment and reward in themselves. Do *not* give a reward if the dog performs some desirable behavior of his own volition, but only after a command. Never become too short-tempered with a young dog—your mood may upset the animal.

Teaching the **basic behaviors**

Most dog owners won't be taking their pets to competitions and don't require them to perform party tricks. Training in basic behaviors is, however, important for the good handling and safe management of the dog throughout its life.

What to train
The basic behaviors to teach your dog are:

- stop and sit (see page 103)
- come when called (see page 105)
- lie down (see page 104)
- stay (see page 106)
- walk to heel (see page 111)
- wait (see page 138)

How to train
Teaching your dog to perform these behaviors on command is not difficult. All you need is patience and time every day to work with your pet. Older dogs take longer to train and may be better taken to professional training classes. Puppies can begin training when they are between three and four months old. Training sessions should last no longer than ten minutes for puppies and 20 minutes for adult dogs. Do not let the dog get bored by training for too long without a break.

Only one person in the family should be involved in training the dog. Do not let other family members interfere with training sessions in order to avoid confusing the animal. They can still play with and praise the dog at other times, and can learn and use the commands later after the dog has been satisfactorily trained.

You will be using verbal commands during training, but if you accompany them each time with some type of visual cue—a gesture with a finger, hand, or arm, a movement of your head, or some such—and are always consistent with your signaling, you will eventually be able to drop the spoken words completely and initiate your pet's responses by visual signals alone. Initially, use a collar and lead as a training aid until you have full verbal control.

Paw research

Researchers at Sydney University, Australia, have found that 15 percent of dogs are right-pawed and 15 percent left-pawed. The remaining 70 percent show no preference, and are generally less bright than those with a preference, are less easy to train, and are more prone to noise phobias. Other experts speculate that paw preference may be influenced by owners, and suggest that dogs that are left-pawed, for example, have been conditioned by commands mostly given by their owners' right hand, and that those without a preference may not have had sufficient interaction with humans while growing up.

Paw preference
Dogs, like us, can be either right- or left-handed, and find some behaviors easier to perform on one side rather than the other. Try to determine by watching if your dog is right- or left-pawed. Help your pet to learn more easily by favoring the preferred side. Later, encourage him in training to be ambidextrous, so that he is more balanced.

Food rewards
It is advisable to use food rewards sparingly in training. Prepare pea-sized pieces of food and accompany them with praise. The best food treats are sausage, lamb's liver, or mild hard cheese. It is vital that rewards are given immediately after the dog responds correctly to a command. Chocolate should not be used, as it contains the chemical theobromine, which is toxic for dogs, particularly toy breeds, and can cause vomiting and diarrhoea or even death at high doses. "Safe" chocolate treats for dogs are available, but are not a healthy option.

Watch

This command is important in enabling you to gain and keep the dog's attention, and thereby progress in teaching him other things. It is a good exercise for beginning every training session.

1 Take a treat and gain your dog's attention by holding it near to your face and speaking or calling his name until he looks at you. Make sure he knows this is a treat you are showing him—if necessary, bring it close to his face for a few seconds and then take it away.

2 Wait a few seconds with the treat held high, keeping his attention. At this stage, your dog may even sit for you, but don't worry if he doesn't. Holding his attention is the important thing. Reward him with the treat if he remains focused on you and the treat, and pet him so that he knows you are pleased.

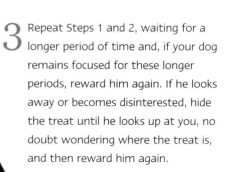

3 Repeat Steps 1 and 2, waiting for a longer period of time and, if your dog remains focused for these longer periods, reward him again. If he looks away or becomes disinterested, hide the treat until he looks up at you, no doubt wondering where the treat is, and then reward him again.

Sit

Once your dog understands the "Sit" command, use it every time before giving the dog something he wants, such as a toy or a walk outside. The Sit position is used at certain stages in other training procedures. However, dogs with hip joint problems, such as dysplasia and arthritis, should not be asked to sit for long periods of time during training.

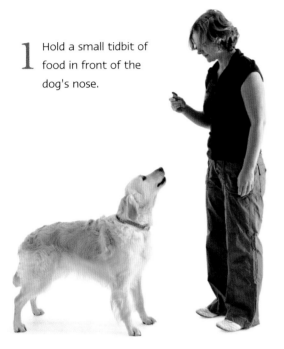

1 Hold a small tidbit of food in front of the dog's nose.

2 Move it slowly and steadily up and over his head. The dog's nose will almost always follow the lure upwards, while his rear end moves down to the floor and into the Sit position.

3 As his bottom makes contact with the floor, say "Sit" and give him the titbit. Do not hold the food too high or the dog may jump up for it instead of sitting. After several repeat performances, you should find that merely sweeping your hand upwards without a food morsel will produce the Sit response.

Down

As with the "Sit" command (see page 103), it will not take many repetitions of this exercise before your hand movement alone, without the tidbit, will evoke the correct response.

1 Begin with the dog in the Sit position, ideally on a smooth, but not too slippery surface, rather than a carpet or rug. Show the dog the treat.

2 Move the treat downwards from in front of the tip of his nose to the floor immediately in front of his toes. If it is too far away, you may stimulate him to stand and walk toward the food.

3 When his front end eases down onto the floor, say "Down" and give the food reward.

Come

This is best achieved with a long leash—the extendable "fishing reel" kind, or by attaching 33–50 ft (10–15 m) of nylon cord to your regular lead. Do not scold him if he does not come on the odd occasion. Instead, lavish praise upon him when he does come. During the off-lead training, you can try turning away as you give the command. This plays on a dog's pack instinct.

1 Ask your dog to **Sit** (see page 103), and when he does, turn and walk a few steps away.

2 Once you are a few feet away, turn and call the dog by name and say "**Come**" emphatically. If he is hesitant in responding, give a gentle tug on the leash and retract it to take up the slack.

3 Keep calling and praising him as he comes toward you. Give the dog lots of praise and reward him for responding.

4 When the dog seems ready, you can dispense with the leash. If, however, he subsequently refuses to come or sits just out of range, go back to lead training.

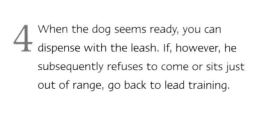

Stay

Once your dog will sit on command, you must introduce "Stay." You should also practice the similar combination of "Down–Stay." Eventually, you can turn this type of obedience training into a game by giving the commands in a variety of positions and places in order to reinforce the dog's essential understanding of the words. Say "Sit" or "Down" when you are standing with your back to the dog, with your eyes closed, when you are lying down, or cooking a meal. Then go on to give a series of different commands. Fulsome praise should be a sufficient reward for correct compliance. Dogs seem to enjoy this sort of opportunity to please you and show that they know what you are saying.

1 With your dog walking to heel on the leash (see page 111), stop, make him sit (see page 103), and turn to face him.

2 Command "**Stay**" while extending one arm away from your body, palm upwards, toward the dog (for the dog, this psychologically reduces the distance between you). Walk one step away from him, still with your hand held out. If the dog moves to come to you, stop the exercise and return close to him. If he stays, reward him and go on to Step 3.

3 Move two steps away from the dog. Keep your hand held out, saying "Stay."

4 Now try the "**Sit-Stay**" command without the leash, gradually increasing your distance from the dog. You can develop the command by turning your back to your dog and also going further away until you are out of sight. When you return, praise your dog for his obedience and walk on.

Take and give

Take and Give combined with Hold and Drop (see page 109) form part of the retrieve behavior outlined on page 114. Older dogs in particular should learn these commands before going on to retrieve training. You will need to be patient—training can take anything between a few days, and a few weeks. The object used can be a toy or a ball, but best of all is a toy dumbbell of a size that fits neatly across the dog's jaws.

1 Put the dog into the Sit position beside your left leg (see page 103). Gently open his mouth by putting the palm of your left hand under his mouth and inserting your thumb between the lips behind his canine (fang) tooth.

2 When the mouth is open, put the object in it with your right hand and say "**Take**." Close the mouth by gently clasping it with your right hand.

3 Give him lots of praise, say "**Give**" and at once take the object out of the mouth. Give a food reward and more praise. Repeat the sequence six to ten times during each of six daily training sessions.

Hold and drop

This exercise begins in the same way as the Take and Give lesson (see page 108). Don't forget to give him praise both while holding and dropping after being given the command.

1 Put the dog into the Sit position beside your left leg (see page 103). Gently open his mouth by putting the palm of your left hand under his muzzle or mouth and inserting your thumb between the lips behind his canine (fang) tooth.

2 When the mouth is open, put the object in it with your right hand and say "**Take**." Close the mouth by gently clasping it with your right hand, hold it closed, and say "**Hold**."

3 Praise him and, then, after only a second or two, release your grip and say "**Drop**." Give praise and a food treat as soon as the dog drops the object. Repeat the procedure, but no more than two or three times while keeping the mouth closed for several seconds longer.

Combining take, hold, and drop

Once you have mastered this combination exercise, you can move on to the full retrieve sequence shown on page 114. Make sure you use a suitable toy that your dog can safely hold in his mouth.

1 Make the object you are using more tempting by smearing it with some meat paste or cream cheese. Hold it close to the dog's nose and say "**Take**." He is almost certain to start licking the object. As he does so, sneak the object into his mouth.

2 Give praise and say "**Drop**." As soon as he drops it, give praise and a treat.

3 Repeat the procedure but also say "**Hold**" as you slip the object into his mouth. Continue the repetitions until he voluntarily takes the object out of your hand, but begin to move a little further away from him each time before giving the "Take" command. When the dog will reliably come and take from a distance of 3 ft (1 m), continue the repetitions but gradually lower the target object each time he does a successful "Take" on command until he will eventually retrieve it from the floor at his feet.

Walking to heel

A 6-7 ft (2 m) long leash is best, with only about 1 m (3 ft) of it being used, the rest held in reserve. Put the leash on the dog, speaking reassuringly and calmly. Hold it firmly in one or both hands. The leash must never be taut. Make any turns carefully and always turn right, away from the dog (turning left may make him worry about becoming entangled in your legs). Introduce left turns only when he is accustomed to walking on the leash.

1 Shorten the leash and bring the dog into the required position with his right shoulder beside your left leg.

2 Begin to walk in a straight line, saying "Heel" firmly as you start. Continue talking pleasantly to your dog to reassure him that all is well.

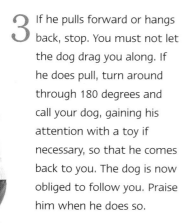

3 If he pulls forward or hangs back, stop. You must not let the dog drag you along. If he does pull, turn around through 180 degrees and call your dog, gaining his attention with a toy if necessary, so that he comes back to you. The dog is now obliged to follow you. Praise him when he does so.

4 As he comes back to you, bring his head level with your knee and turn him around to the right. Keep him moving around, so that he is not tempted to sit. If necessary, give him verbal encouragement to keep him moving. Continue to walk in the direction and at the pace you were originally going.

Anti-pulling strategies

It is important that your dog learns to walk to heel at your side on a lead without pulling. Dogs that pull are actually training their owners rather than the other way around. Powerfully built breeds, such as Chow Chows and Huskies, can indulge in strenuous pulling. For such dogs, and old dogs, a halter-collar and leash or, better still, a harness with training leashes attached to both ends, is advisable. Gentle, not violent, tugs on the leash turn the dog's head when using a halter-collar, and small, frequent tugs on both leashes when using a harness help to keep the dog in check. When the dog pulls, the owner should give the tug and change the direction of walk. Throughout the training process, a pocketful of treats and fulsome praise must be available with which to reward the animal as he stops pulling and walks easily alongside.

Training youngsters

Young dogs particularly may be frightened of the lead to begin with. Put on the leash when feeding him in the home and let him trail it around—one about 6 ft (1.8 m) long is best, but not the retractable kind at this stage. When you first go out for a walk, avoid pulling hard on the leash if the dog is unwilling to move and hangs back, as this will only frighten him further. Walk ahead of the animal to the full extent of the leash, bend down or crouch on your haunches, clap your hands once, and praise the dog. The tone of your voice must be reassuring and happy, with no trace of impatience or irritation. If he does not move, give the leash a gentle tug or two. Should this fail, change the direction of walk by going behind the dog and repeating the procedure crouched in that position. When the dog responds, give a food reward immediately. A daily practice session will usually have a youngster walking contentedly to heel within a week.

Advanced training

Further training and your subsequent maintenance of the behaviors your dog has learned through frequent repetition will actually improve his intelligence, as well as providing both of you with pleasure, fun, and exercise.

Rollover

With practice, the dog will roll without the need to follow the food lure, the visual cue can be reduced to a finger moved and the verbal command omitted. Give him the food treat together with a longer tummy rub when he has completed the rollover perfectly. Some breeds, such as Great Danes, are too big for this exercise, so should not be encouraged to do it.

1 Put your dog into the "Down-Stay" position (see pages 104 and 106). Hold a morsel of food directly under his nose. As he sniffs it and gets interested, slowly bring the food over his back. His head will follow your hand.

2 When the food is over his back, he will shift his body to one side. As he does this, give the command "Roll!" Move your hand and the food over to the side he is now lying on.

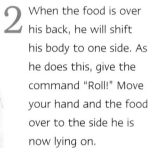

3 He may try to bring his head to the food from the opposite direction. If he does, move your hand to the other side, gently pushing his body toward the food. When he has successfully changed sides, give him the food treat and lots of praise.

4 Soon the dog will follow the food lure and roll correctly. Praise him and give him a short tummy rub, but wait until he sits up before giving the treat. Now you can use a visual cue, such as a downward-winding motion of your hand and arm, with the verbal command.

Fetch

If your dog is not one of the naturally retrieving breeds, this can be a fairly difficult behavior to train. Use a plastic toy, such as a dumbbell or bone. Do not use pieces of branches, which may carry spikes or splinters that could injure your dog's mouth.

Puppy training

It is best, if possible, to begin training with a puppy; most love running after and retrieving balls, sticks, and toys. When a puppy voluntarily retrieves an object and proudly brings it back to you, make sure that you praise his skill and enthusiasm generously. But do not wrench it from his mouth—he must lay or drop it in front of you. He will soon learn that you will not throw the object again unless he gives it up.

Now throw an object and say "Fetch." When he returns, say "Good boy" and then "Drop." Pick up the object and give him more praise. Once he has firmly grasped the idea, say "Fetch" together with the name of the object, such as "Fetch the toy." Begin to use two or three different objects in the game, say a ball, a toy, and a rubber bone. This way, he will soon begin to learn the names of objects and how to discriminate between them.

Training older dogs

Older dogs may not automatically retrieve things as easily as puppies, so it is often best to train them first in Take and give (see page 108) and Hold and drop (see page 109). When the dog will reliably pick up the target object from the floor at his feet, progressively place it further and further away: 1 ft (30 cm), 3 ft (1 m) and then 6½ ft (2 m). Do no more than six repetitions in a session to avoid boredom.

Now throw the object a short distance and say "Fetch." Praise him when he picks it up. When he brings it back to you, say "Give" and reward with a food treat and more praise. If he fools around or runs off with the object, give the "Come" command as soon as he picks up the object and give him praise and a treat when he obeys and comes to you. Gradually increase the throwing distance and, if you wish, introduce the "Sit" and "Hold" when he gets back.

Catching in the air

Pastoral dogs, such as the Border Collie and Australian Shepherd Dog, are generally skilled at air catching. Dogs that find catching balls in the air rather difficult often do much better with flatter objects such as Frisbees. If using a ball, make sure that it is big enough not to be swallowed or get stuck in the back of the dog's throat.

Have your dog about 6½ ft (2 m) in front of you in the Sit–Stay position (see pages 103 and 106). Throw the ball and, at the same time, give the "Fetch" command. If he catches it, give praise; if he does not, hold the ball above his head and tease him with it. When he jumps up for it, let him take it in his mouth and then give praise. Repeat at short distances away until he successfully catches the ball every time. Gradually increase the distance between you and begin throwing the ball not directly toward him but in another direction. With each successful catch, very gradually increase the height and distance of your throw.

Tidying up

Once your dog is solidly trained to fetch a variety of objects, you can soon get him to put them tidily away. Scatter a number of your pet's toys and favorite "personal belongings" on the floor. Get the dog to pick them up one at a time and bring them to you, placing them in your hand rather than dropping them at your feet, prompting him with the command "Give." Put the objects in a nearby box or bin and give the dog a food treat reward for each "gift" he brings you. Some very sharp dogs will soon go further by retrieving the object and dropping it straight in the box.

Diet and dog intelligence

Can dogs eat themselves bright? It would seem so. Considering exactly what you give your dog to eat, adjusting certain features of its diet, and providing certain supplements have been proved to have an enhancing effect on canine intelligence.

The role of omega fatty acids

It is well known that diet can influence intelligence levels in babies and growing children. The fatty acid content of food, particularly of the one called omega 3 found in fish, especially salmon, mackerel, and herring, is important if children are to attain their optimum IQ level. It seems that something similar may well apply to dogs. The exact role of omega 3 in canine nutrition is not completely understood, but it does appear to play an important part in brain function. Too much omega 3 in the diet, however, can lead to health problems. Another fatty acid, omega 6, found in sunflower, corn, and other plant oils, pork and poultry fat, but occurring in negligible amounts in beef and butter fat, is also essential for dogs. Proprietary pet foods generally supply enough omega 6 through their content of corn and chicken fat.

Health conditions attributed to fatty-acid deficiency in dogs include skin ailments, hair loss, weakness, circulatory disorders, and poor wound healing, as well as impairment of vision and learning ability.

Dietary principles

To avoid faulty nutrition affecting their pets, owners should ensure a broad diet at all ages, and especially for pregnant and lactating bitches in order to protect brain development in their puppies. Canned and other kinds of "complete" proprietary dog foods are fine, but if you assemble your pet's meals yourself, be sure always to include a good variety of meats, lean and fatty, vegetables, and carbohydrates in the form of biscuits or meal. Supplements containing omega fatty acids are available. All-biscuit diets or low-meat and -fat regimes will adversely affect your dog, mentally and physically.

Food puzzles

One excellent way of improving your dog's intelligence, while at the same time relieving any between-meal boredom by exercising both his mind and body as well as feeding him, is to provide him with food puzzles. A fairly recent development, this technique consists in essence of replacing the dog's food bowl with a variety of food puzzles that are hidden around the house, under a bed or behind a sofa. This allows your pet to snack on his ration of food throughout the day instead of wolfing it all down in 30 seconds. Animal behaviorists believe that these food-motivated exercises result in pets that are physically healthier, smarter, and more emotionally fulfilled.

Food-puzzle feeding is ideal for the dog owner who goes out to work, because it provides a simple way of keeping the dog occupied while it is alone, and will reduce the chances of it becoming bored and destructive.

Types of food puzzle

The food-puzzle devices themselves are toys, usually made of stout plastic or rubber, in which pieces of food can be concealed, and come in a wide range of designs, presenting the dog trying to get at his victuals with varying degrees of fiendishness. They can be purchased at pet stores or on the Internet, and it is best to obtain two or three different ones, which can then be used in rotation. Examples are the Buster Cube, a large hollow dice with apertures, and the Dog Tornado, which has four rotating disks, three of which have compartments for food.

Some food puzzles are adjustable and can be customized to your dog's weight, experience, and personality.

How to use

It is best to give leaner dogs, such as Greyhounds, and those that are easily frustrated or just beginning the easier puzzles. Once the easy puzzles have been mastered, and for overweight and sharp-witted characters, provide harder puzzles. Canned dog food is best frozen before being put inside the puzzles. The puzzles should be placed in a pan or large dish to avoid making a mess on your floor when the dog gets to work.

Toy treats

If you prefer to feed your dog in the traditional way from a bowl, there are lots of puzzle toys available which dispense treats and that you can use on a less-routine basis. Again of varying degrees of difficulty, they exercise the dog's mind and reward it with small morsels rather than portions of his basic diet. Kongs are small puzzle toys made of vulcanized rubber that can be stuffed with treats and, for the lonely dog, there are Kong Dispensers that contain four Kongs and release one at intervals throughout the day!

Squeaky puzzles

Finally, there are the puzzle toys that do not dispense edible treats at all, but squeaky ones instead. You can, for example, find a nest from which the dog has to extract squeaking squirrels, a hive containing squeaking bees, and a soft plush bone from which your pet has to remove a number of squeaking rings.

Clever games and tricks

Regular physical and mental activity keeps the dog's body and brain in optimum condition, strengthens the relationship between owner and pet, and is a source of constant enjoyment for both. The exercises that follow, even the more advanced, are based on the same basic principles of training presented in the previous chapter, which can be adapted to teach your pet all manner of useful behaviors. We have all heard of dogs that act as reliable alarm clocks, fetch slippers, newspapers, car keys, or other articles whose names they have memorized, or open doors. I know of one Tervueren that promptly brings a box of paper tissues when his owner sneezes!

Certain of the tricks that follow are more difficult to train than others, and a significant percentage of dogs will not be able to learn all of them. Some of the more energetic games and training are obviously not well suited to, say, an arthritic Dachshund living in a tenth-floor apartment in an inner-city block. Nevertheless, with a little thought on the part of owners, something can be done to sharpen the wits of all pet dogs, whatever their level of intelligence, physical capabilities, and circumstances.

Advanced treasure hunt

Effect Toys or other objects are hidden from the dog, which he then retrieves and returns to you.

Good for Enhances a dog's natural hunting and tracking abilities, and can be enjoyed indoors or out.

Which breed? Hunting and tracking breeds are usually very quick if the object is one of their familiar toys, as they know its scent. Dogs with better vision and less scenting skill, such as the sight hounds, will tend to be slower. For them, and pets that do not possess a favorite toy, a food treat (with its stronger smell) can be used as the retrieve object.

1 Begin by using the dog's favorite toy. Throw it to a short distance away and then gradually increase the distance. Repeat until he reliably retrieves it each time.

2 Hide the object where it can be easily found, but in full view of your pet, after giving him the "Sit-Stay" commands (see pages 103 and 106). Go back to the dog and command "Find it." When he returns with the object, give praise and, in the early stages, a food treat.

3 Gradually increase the difficulty of finding the object, first by putting it partly behind the chair, tree, or whatever, and, subsequently, completely out of sight.

4 When the dog is proficient, go on to hide the object when you are out of his sight (put him indoors or out as appropriate). Then, when you let him join you again, say "Find it."

Nose flip

Effect   A treat is balanced on the dog's nose and then flipped into the air and caught in his mouth.

Good for   This trick both demonstrates and enhances a dog's coordination, and also helps to sharpen the dog's intelligence. It is not a particularly easy behavior to teach.

Which breed?   The dog that is most proficient at this in my experience is a friend's Borzoi playing with his master's credit card! Conversely, this is not a trick for the likes of Pugs, Pekingeses, and Bulldogs.

1 With the dog sitting in front of you, throw him treats or toys for him to catch, giving praise and a treat if he is successful. If he misses, try to retrieve the object before he can, particularly if using food treats, to prevent him being rewarded for failure. When he seldom misses, start using the command "Catch."

2 Use the "Sit–Stay" commands (see pages 103 and 106) to place your dog in a sitting position with him looking at you but with his nose level. Gently place the object on his nose. Make sure it is balanced and not too close to his eyes. Repeat the "Stay" command. Wait a moment, remove the object, and give praise and a treat. Repeat several times.

3 Balance the object on the dog's nose and, as he watches you, pretend to throw him something while giving the "Catch" command. Hopefully, he will lift his muzzle up and the object will fall off. Praise and reward when he does. Repeat until he catches the dislodged object—it can take many repetitions before the dog understands what is required. Then, of course, give fulsome praise and a treat.

Sit up and beg

Effect   The dog sits on his bottom with his body upright, with both paws held off the ground.

Good for   Teaches obedience to command as well as improving balance.

Which breed?   This behavior can be rather difficult for dogs with longish bodies and short legs, such as Dachshunds and Basset Hounds, but much easier for stockier-built types, like terriers and spaniels. It is best avoided in dogs that have had slipped-disc or other spinal problems.

1 Stand in front of your dog with him in the Sit–Stay position (see pages 103 and 106). Hold a food treat directly above his head and fairly close to his nose so that he is not tempted to jump for it. Give the command "Beg" and at the same time extend the index finger of the hand holding the treat to form a visual cue.

2 As he starts to reach for the treat, raise it so that it is just a little too high for him. When he raises a paw off the ground, give praise and the treat.

3 Repeat the procedure, but this time when he lifts the paw, use one hand to lift his paw higher and with the other hand continue luring him upwards with the treat. The dog will raise his other paw. Praise and give the treat.

4 After several repetitions when the dog is fully accustomed to using your hand as a support when he sits up, begin gradually drawing your hand away from him while still luring him upward.

Shaking hands and waving

Effect   The dog holds out a paw to be shaken, but then goes on to make a pawing movement in the air, as if waving.

Good for   Teaches obedience to command and impresses visitors.

Which breed?   Teaching any dog to hold out a paw is relatively easy—it is one of the animal's natural placatory gestures of submission. Bigger breeds, such as the retrievers and pastoral dogs (see pages 66–67), are the best at waving, although I have known some very skilled and enthusiastic terrier wavers!

1 With your dog in the Sit position (see page 103), sit on the ground, too, or bend down to him if you are in a chair. Stretch out your hand, palm upwards, and say "Paw" or "Shake." As the dog raises his paw, take it gently and shake it. Praise the dog when he does so and reward with a treat. Repeat four or five times.

2 Repeat the same command but, just as the dog stretches out his paw toward your hand, lift it upwards just beyond his reach. He will then extend his limb a little further in order to touch your hand. When he does so, give praise and a treat.

3 Using the same command, delay the reward until he tries to touch your hand by giving a little pawing movement in the air. Very soon he should reach out twice and then three times. Vary the height at which you hold your hand to strengthen the behavior. Do not make the dog lift his paw too high, or he may need to put the paw down in order to regain balance. Once the dog is reliably making a definite wave, give the command "Wave" instead of "Paw" or "Shake."

Taking a bow

Effect   The dog lowers the front half of his body to the ground as if bowing.

Good for   Teaches obedience to command and impresses visitors.

Which breed?   Breeds such as the Corgi, Dachshund, and Boxer should not be encouraged to do this exercise, and it certainly must not be attempted by any dog that has had spinal problems, such as a slipped disc.

1 Have the dog stand in front of you, preferably with you sitting on the floor. With the palm of your hand upwards, hold a treat to his nose. Move the treat downwards and forwards as if intending to put it under his chest. The aim is to get his nose to tilt down and back as it follows the treat, and so induce him to lower his forequarters. As soon as he begins to dip (you must be quick and do it before he drops into a fully Down position), praise and reward.

2 Repeat, very gradually extending the time before you give the praise and treat reward so that he keeps dropping further. Eventually, he will drop down onto his elbows while keeping his hindquarters raised. At this point give the command "Bow" before rewarding.

3 Repeat the procedure in order to link the command firmly to the behavior, and then do the trick with you kneeling and standing. When the dog will confidently perform the bow to your verbal command, stop using the food treat.

Jumping hurdles

Effect Like a human hurdling athlete, the dog runs and jumps over one or more barriers.

Good for Improves physical and mental fitness.

Which breed? The best breeds at hurdling are the longer-legged hounds (see pages 64–65), gundogs (see pages 76–77) and some pastoral breeds, such as the German Shepherd Dog and collies (see pages 66–67). Puppies should not be taught to jump in this way, because their bones and joints can easily be injured.

1 Construct a low hurdle that your dog can walk over and put him on a long leash. Walk your dog at heel over the hurdle several times in both directions.

2 Place your dog on one side of the hurdle in the Sit–Stay position (see pages 103 and 106) and go to the other side. Call the dog to come to you. As he approaches the hurdle, give the command "Jump" and begin to walk backwards while reeling in his leash.

3 When he has jumped over, have him sit facing you and give plenty of praise. Continue in this manner over several sessions until you feel he does not need the lead to guide him. Stay on the other side of the hurdle when you call him, and let him jump and come to sit in front of you.

4 When the dog is reliable in performing the jump on command, begin increasing the height of the hurdle gradually by 1–2 in (2.5–5 cm) increments, but do not set the height at more than one and a half times the dog's own height.

Talking dog

Effect In this entertaining trick, the dog is instructed to "speak" on cue by barking.

Good for Teaches obedience to command and can progress to responding to a variety of signals, some quite subtle.

Which breed? Some dogs go in for barking more than others and so are easier to train in this behavior. Particularly good barking breeds are terriers, working dogs (see pages 72–73), and utility dogs (see pages 70–71) and terrier-type mongrels (see page 78). Obviously, the trick does not work well with the barkless Basenji breed!

1 Have your dog in a Sit-Stay position (see pages 103 and 106) while you stand in front of him and hold either a favorite toy or a food treat above his head. Tempt and tease him with the object, waggling it and talking to him about it in an eager tone of voice, then repeat a command word such as "Speak," but do not let him have it.

2 When the dog begins to make a noise of any kind or move his lips or get excited, give him praise and the toy or treat.

3 Continue in the same way, but only give the reward when he intensifies his response by making more sounds or moving his mouth more. Build progressively on each "Speak" command until the dog, usually within the space of only a few repetitions, makes the connection and emits a noise immediately on receiving the verbal cue. Try adding a visual cue to your verbal command, such as a finger movement or a nod of your head, so that the verbal command can be dispensed with.

Digging

Effect   The dog digs up an object that you have buried and then, if you are lucky and he is well-trained, buries it again.

Good for   Encourages problem solving and involves physical exercise. Can be bad for herbaceous borders!

Which breed?   I have found dogs, by and large, to be keener diggers than buriers, and that very much includes terriers!

1 Show the dog one of his toys and then bury it, with him watching you. As you bury it, repeat the word "Bury" several times. Now stand aside and let him dig it up and bring the toy to you. Praise him when he does.

2 Then say "Bury" and wait for him to bury his toy. This needs lots of encouragement, as well as praise, if it is achieved. Most dogs, but especially terriers, of course, will do this very naturally.

Obstacle course

Effect Like the assault courses used in training soldiers and marines, this is a series of obstacles that the dog must overcome.

Good for Provides much fun for the dog, instills confidence, and promotes physical agility.

Which breed? Any breed except short-legged types like Dachshunds, and, of course, unsuitable for those with arthritis or other handicaps.

If you have access to a spare piece of land or a large yard, and possess the basic minimum of handicraft skills, constructing an obstacle course for your dog can be very worthwhile, particularly once he has learned to jump on command. Dogs love to use these "fun runs." Build the obstacles in your course using material that cannot injure your dog—no jagged edges or protrusions, or toxic paint. Structures should be stable, but with the bars on hurdles loose so that they will fall easily if clipped by a foot. Features of the obstacle course can include:

Old, large diameter tire Hang it suspended by several ropes coming from different directions so that it barely moves.

Tunnel Make by covering half hoops or angled sticks with paper, sheets, or wooden board, large enough for the dog to pass through easily; begin with one about 3 ft (1 m) long, which can be increased in time. Introduce bends.

Ramp A slatted wooden plane that, at first, should rise to about 2 ft (60 cm) high

Hurdle No higher than the height to which the dog has been jumping during training. When you take the dog out to the course, use all the familiar commands as appropriate. Encourage him to pass through or over each obstacle by luring with a toy or food treats and enthusiastic verbal and body language on your part. Accompany him all the way through and reward him with plenty of praise and treats when he has finished the course. If necessary, at first use the long leash as you did for hurdle jumping. Most dogs get the idea of the obstacle course very quickly and tackle it with obvious relish.

As the dog becomes experienced, make the tunnel more fiendish in design and length, raise the ramp angle, and install a second tire and hurdle.

Hide and seek

Effect A doggy version of the children's party game of Hide and Seek.

Good for Encourages the dog to use all of its senses in trying to find you.

Which breed? All breeds, but especially the Toy and Terrier groups.

This is a game for indoors, not out in a busy park. Give the dog the "Sit-Stay" commands (see pages 103 and 106), then go off and find a hiding place, just as in a children's game of hide and seek.

When you have found it, call the dog by name, repeating it if you can tell he is moving in the wrong direction. When he discovers you, give a treat and lots of praise.

Keep your **old dog** smart

As with humans, approaching old age can bring changes in the minds, and therefore the apparent intelligence, of dogs. The frontal lobes of the brain are involved in many fundamental functions, including problem solving, memory, judgment, initiation, and social and sexual behavior. Dogs' frontal lobes begin to shrink with approaching old age usually at somewhere between eight and eleven years, when the first signs of senile behavior changes may appear.

Gradually, progressive degenerative processes within brain cells can begin from as early as seven years of age, and these tend to affect the animal's cognitive abilities. When established, the condition, called canine cognitive dysfunction (CCD), is associated with human pathological changes in the brain that are markedly similar to those found in Alzheimer's disease. In the dog, the symptoms, too, can be similar to those of the human condition (see page 139).

But how can we prevent or at least reduce the speed of onset-of-old-age changes in the dog's brain or help ameliorate them if they already exist? This chapter focuses in turn on the three main aspects of effective action that a dog owner can take: physical activity, mental simulation, and adjustment of diet.

Understanding the
ageing issues

Dogs do show physical changes with the passing years. Mental faculties don't necessarily deteriorate in senior human or canine citizens, but sometimes old dogs begin to show signs similar to those seen in human patients. If it happens, all is not lost. Owners can take steps to alleviate the condition.

Veterinary attention

It is most important to remember that signs of cognitive dysfunction may *not* be age-related or caused by brain degeneration, but instead indicate disease or malfunction somewhere else in the body. For example, a dog developing deafness may appear disobedient, but simply be missing your commands. Fading sight may make performing tricks difficult, and arthriticky animals are understandably disinclined to engage in much physical activity.

In all cases, veterinary attention should be obtained at the first sign of any such symptoms or if other signs of health problems occur. Many of them, including certain types of eye and ear disease, can be successfully treated or at least alleviated, and all elderly dogs will benefit from having a regular check up at the veterinarian's every six months or, if you see your dog beginning to lose weight, every three months.

Continuing communication

As previously explained, it is vital to communicate with your dog through both words and body language (see pages 98–99). This ensures that if your pet does become deaf in later life, it can still *see* what you are "saying" and the "conversation" between you can continue unhindered throughout the rest of its life.

Age limits

The world's oldest known dog, an Australian Cattle Dog, died at the age of over 29 in 2000. Also from Australia, there is an unsubstantiated claim that a dog named Bluey, a Queensland "heeler," lived for 29 years and five months, eventually dying in 1940.

It is a commonly held belief that one year of a dog's life is equivalent to seven of a man's. That is not so. If it were, a man who had attained the age of the aforementioned Bluey would have celebrated his 203rd birthday! There is no simple multiplier, but the following is a fairly accurate guide for adult dogs:

	Middle Age	Elderly	Geriatric
Man	45–69 years	60–74 years	Over 75 years
Dog: Under 20 lb (9 kg)	c. 7 years	c. 11 years	c. 15 years
20–50 lb (9–23 kg)	c. 7 years	c. 10 years	c. 14 years
Over 50 lb (23 kg)	c. 5 years	c. 9 years	c. 12 years

Physical **activity**

An important aid in keeping an older dog's brain functioning well is physical activity. Obviously, the owner plays a vital role in providing this. Another key player in helping the old timer to stay mentally young can be a puppy. Exercise promotes fitness not only of the ageing body, but also the brain by increasing the flow of nourishment to the nerve cells. A puppy's presence also exercises the older dog's brain by stimulating thought as well as encouraging it into physical activity.

Routine exercise

Regular, varied exercise is essential for the older dog. Not just the occasional walk on the lead down to the local shops and back, but brisk walks, allowing your pet to run free off the lead in parks or on common land for at least 15 minutes once or twice a day, opportunities to play with other dogs, swimming when possible, and, most important of all, playing games and having fun with you. However, do not overexercise an old dog to the point of him being tired, and do not let him get cold. Games and exercise should take place *before* the feeding time. Fortunately, when the weather is bad outside, there are lots of games that are both mentally and physically stimulating that dog and owner can play together indoors.

Puppy therapy

Bringing a young puppy into the household where an older dog is already a family member is invaluable in keeping an "old-timer" in good shape. All the activity improves the animal's physical condition as well as stimulating better circulation of blood to the brain. The enhanced production of chemicals are beneficial to and protective of brain function. The production of serotonin, an anti-depressant and good mood booster, is especially stimulated by puppy therapy.

Diet and the **ageing dog**

There are ways of slowing the onset of cognitive dysfunction in dogs and in combatting it if it has already begun to develop. Attention to the diet and the provision of certain nutritional supplements are important methods of doing this.

Intelligence-preserving supplements

Nowadays, there is a plethora of advice from the mass media about improving and modifying our diets, as well as a wealth of health-promoting products. Much, but not all, has a scientific basis, and the same can be said about many of the proprietary foods and food supplements for pets.

Throughout their lives, all dogs must have a good, nutritious, balanced diet, but beyond six or seven years of age, certain constituents become important, particularly in combating the brain changes mentioned earlier (see page 134). Vitamins, anti-oxidants, and mitochondrial co-factors (the latter help brain neurons to function better and cut the production of free radicals) bring real, lasting benefits.

Owners should try to include the following in their older dogs' diet:

* Small quantities of fruit and vegetables
* Vitamin E—small dog 500 mgs, medium-sized dog 800 mgs, large dog 1,000 mgs daily
* Vitamin C—20 mgs per 2 lb (1 kg) dog body weight daily
* Carnitine and alpha-lipoic acid (mitochondrial co-factors), obtainable separately or in a combined form from health food shops and some pharmacies—medium-sized dog minimum daily dose of 50 mgs alpha-lipoic acid, 250 mgs carnitine

Other supplements worth considering are the fatty acids containing omega 6 (see page 116), also available in the form of fish oil capsules. As an alternative, feed your dog some cooked oily fish, such as herring or mackerel, once a week.

Scientific endorsement

A fascinating experiment was carried out on four groups of 7- to 11-year-old Beagles. After being subjected to intelligence tests, one group (A) received extra exercise and mental stimulation, together with a normal diet supplemented with tomato, carrot granules, citrus pulp, spinach flakes, vitamins E and C, alpha-lipoic acid, and carnitine. A second group (B) received a normal diet supplemented as aforementioned but without the extra exercise and mental stimulation. A third group (C) received a normal diet without supplementation but with extra exercise and mental stimulation. The fourth group (D) received only the normal diet. After some weeks, when the dogs were retested, Group D showed no change in IQ, Groups B and C both did equally much better, while Group A was by far the most improved. When this experiment was carried out on young Beagles, however, there was no change in any of the groups' IQs. This suggests that dietary supplementation has a therapeutic effect in older animals and is therefore well worth giving to dogs that have already begun to show signs of mental deterioration.

Dutch scientists have demonstrated that daily doses of folic acid, the vitamin found naturally in green leafy vegetables, beans, and liver, can set back the effects of ageing on the human brain by five years. A similar effect may well take place in old dogs given folic-acid supplements.

Although these supplements may not be cheap, and assembling them with the other ingredients of the recommended diet may take a little time, the results should be much better than those obtained by feeding "supplemented" proprietary canned or pelleted foods marketed for older animals.

Fighting canine flab

Recently, it has been suggested by medical scientists that being significantly overweight, because of its effects in reducing blood circulation within, and nutrition of, the brain, can reduce the intelligence of human beings. The same may very well apply to dogs and be another reason, besides reducing the risks of diabetes, circulatory, and joint troubles in later life, for stopping our pets from becoming obese. A drug called Slentrol designed to combat canine obesity has now been made available in the U.S. and will be introduced elsewhere. However, side effects, such as vomiting, diarrhea, and even anorexia, have been reported. Controlling your pet's diet and giving regular exercise remains a safer, cheaper way to keep excess weight at bay.

Mental stimulation

The fitness of a brain depends upon it being kept active just as much as the muscles of the body. It is the owner's responsibility to continually stimulate the dog's brain activity by training the animal to do a variety of things that it has to think about.

Everyday challenges

Getting your dog's brain to exercise depends almost wholly on regular owner involvement. The dog must be given interesting, enjoyable problems to solve, tricks to perform, and games to play (see pages 120–131). But most importantly, you must keep *talking* to your dog regularly and often (see pages 98–99).

Training visually impaired dogs

A blind or severely visually impaired dog can be trained and taught to play and solve problems like a fully sighted one. This will help to reduce his stress, promote his confidence, and help keep him out of trouble. You will need to be patient and *never* give any hint of exasperation. In addition to "Sit" (see page 103), the other key basic commands to teach are:

- **"Slow down"** Necessary to avoid the dog bumping into things. Put the dog on a lead and, when he begins to walk, pull back gently and steadily without jerking while giving the command "Slow down." When he does so correctly, say "Yes!" and reward with fulsome praise and a food treat.
- **"Wait"** An important command that will keep the dog out of danger, for example, when crossing a road. It should not be taught until the "Slow down" has been mastered. Attach the lead and pull back gently but firmly while saying "Wait." Reward when the dog complies immediately.

Training deaf dogs

Deaf dogs can also be trained, and body language is invaluable in communicating (see pages 98–99). You can go further and use hand signs, such as those in the *Webster's American Sign Language Dictionary*. Some deaf dogs have formed a "vocabulary" of up to 50 signs by five or six years of age!

To get the dog's attention, wave your arm, stamp your foot, or flash a pen torch. Training sessions should last no longer than 15 minutes. Although you cannot give vocal praise, the sight of you clapping your hands, smiling, and saying "Good!" expressively will be recognized by the pet.

Coping with **Canine Cognitive Dysfunction** (CCD)

It is now recognized that this condition in old dogs produces behavior changes similar to those in Alzheimer patients. If an owner is faced with a pet showing signs of CCD, there are good ways of coping with and easing the situation.

Symptoms of CCD

These are many and can occur in a variety of combinations and to varying degrees. They include increased sleeping, fewer periods of activity, lack of interest in the outside world, including owners, reduced responsiveness to owners' commands, increased disobedience often manifested as seeming deafness, confusion, difficulty in recognizing familiar humans, forgetting his or her name, lack of appetite, loss of bowel and bladder control, difficulty in navigating familiar environments, "getting lost" in the home, aimless wandering, increased thirst, excessive panting, years of housetraining undone, and episodes of agitation or barking for no apparent reason. A study carried out by veterinarians in the U.S. found that 62 percent of 11- to 16-year-old dogs show one or more of the characteristic signs of CCD.

Medical treatments

Recently, a nonaddictive drug, selegiline hydrochloride, which increases the level of dopamine within the brain, a neurotransmitter chemical involved in transporting nerve messages, and used in the treatment of Parkinson's disease patients, has become available. It reverses many of the signs of brain ageing and strongly boosts cognition and awareness. Two out of three geriatric dogs treated under veterinary supervision have shown significant, even remarkable, improvement in their condition.

It has been found that eradicating parasites, such as round worms, in many cases improves the performance of dogs that have difficulty remembering commands or learning in general. Regular worming or having a teaspoonful of the pet's droppings checked by the vet for the presence of parasites is a sensible precaution for all dog owners.

Practical strategies

Help your dog cope with CCD by ensuring that his environment in and around the home is comfortable, familiar, and friendly:

- Avoid changing or rearranging furniture
- Ensure there are wide, clutter-free walkways throughout
- Consider building or buying a ramp for the staircase to make it easier for the dog to go upstairs
- Form a regular routine of feeding and exercise, with short, gentle play periods
- Keep your commands short, simple, and, above all, considerate
- Be patient and compassionate, and continue to show your pet love and respect for all he has done for you over the years

Bibliography

The mind of the dog

Research by Eotvos Lorand University, Hungary: Vilmos, Csanyi, *If Dogs Could Talk*, Farrar, Strauss & Giroux, 2004

Dr. Edward Wilson's findings on the intelligence of animals: Wallace, Irving: *The Book of Lists No 2*, p 104, William Morrow & Co., 1983

Professor of neuroscience at the University of Witwatersrand, South Africa; theory on dolphins: Manger, Paul R, "An Examination of Cetacean Brain Structure with a Novel Hypothesis Correlating Thermogenesis to the Evolution of a Big Brain," *Biological Review Cambridge Philosophical Society*, 30 March 2006, pp 1–46

Professor Ben Hart, study of dog breeds: Hart, B L, and Miller, M F, "Behavioral Profiles of Dog Breeds," *Journal of the American Veterinary Medical Association*, No 186, 1985, pp 1175–1180

Professor Sam Gosling, University of Texas, test of canine personalities: BBC News, 22 February 2005, "Test for Canine Personalities"

Dr. Susan Eirich quote: www.earthfireinstitute.org, 2003, "Do Animals Have Emotions?"

Leslie Burgard quote: www.leslie@dogsthink.com

Bruce Fogle's survey: Fogle, B, and Abrahamson, D, "Pet Loss: A Survey of the Attitudes and Feelings of Practicing Veterinarians," *Anthrozoos*, Vol 3, No 3, 1990, pp 143–150

Mr Rivera and Dorado: www.moggies.co.uk, "Hero Dog Dorado Saves Blind Owner," 14 September 2001

Dr Belyaev's research: Trut, L N, "Early Canid Domestication: The Fox Farm Experiment," *American Scientist*, No 87, 1999, pp 160–169

Your dog's super senses

Dr. Rupert Sheldrake's experiments: Sheldrake, Rupert, *Dogs That Know When Their Owners Are Coming Home and Other Unexplained Powers of Animals*, Three Rivers Press, 2000

Elizabeth Marshall Thomas quote: Marshall Thomas, Elizabeth, *The Hidden Life of Dogs*, Pocket, reprint edition 1996

Communicating with your dog

Research on vocalization by Eotvos Lorand University, Hungary: Vilmos, Csanyi, *If Dogs Could Talk*, Farrar, Strauss & Giroux, 2004

Turid Rugaas's studies of wolves and dogs: Turid, Rugaas, *On Talking Terms With Dogs: Calming Signals*, 2nd edition, Dogwise Publishing, 2005; *Calming Signals: What Your Dog Tells You*, Dogwise Publishing, 2005

Professor Stanley Coren, *The Intelligence of Dogs*, The Free Press, Hodder Headline, London, 1994

Tim Pennings' experiments: Pennings, T, *College Mathematics Journal*, May 2003

French researchers: Perruchet, P, and Gallego, J, *College Mathematics Journal*, January 2006

Research on long-term memory at the University of Michigan: www.sniksnak.com/cathealth/whydo.html

Dr. Zimen's research into wolves and Poodles: Zimen, E, *The Wolf: A Species in Danger*, Delacorte, 1981; "Ontogeny of Approach and Flight Behavior Toward Humans in Wolves, Poodles, and Wolf Poodle Hybrids," in *Advances, Issues, and Problems in Captive Wolf Research*, (H Frank Edition), Dr. W Junk Publishers, The Netherlands, 1987

Rico, the Border Collie that knows 200 words: Kaminski, J, Call, J, and Fischer, J, "Word Learning in a Domestic Dog: Evidence for 'Fast Mapping'," *Science*, Vol 304, No 5677, 11 June 2004, pp 1682–1683

Quaranta A, Siniscalchi M, and Vallortigara G, "Asymmetric tail-wagging responses by dogs to different emotive stimuli," *Current Biology*, 20 March 2007, pp 199, 17(6)

Making your dog smarter

Research into paw preference by the Sydney University, Australia: *Sunday Telegraph*, 24 December 2006

Keep your old dog smart

Experiment with Beagles: Milgram, N W, Head, E, et. al., "Learning Ability in Aged Beagle Dogs is Preserved by Behavioral Enrichment and Dietary Fortification: A Two-year Longitudinal Study," *Neurobiology of Ageing*, No 26, 2005, pp 77–90

Dutch scientists' research into folic acid: BBC News, 15 August 2005

Training deaf dogs using hand signs: Costello, Elaine, *Webster's American Sign Language Dictionary*, Random House, 1997

Index

Acknowledgments

Author Acknowledgments

Many, many thanks for the help and expertise provided by Trevor Davies, Ruth Hamilton, and Charlotte Macey, my editors at Hamlyn. Also to Joanne Wilson of Octopus with whom I first discussed the idea for this book. And, naturally, to Sid, Golda, Mitzi, Muffin, and Sam, my five Birmans, who draped my computer, desk, and lap in close friendship as I wrote.

Pubisher Acknowledgments

Executive Editor: Trevor Davies
Editor: Charlotte Macey and Ruth Hamilton
Deputy Creative Director: Karen Sawyer
Designers: Pete Gerrish and Mark Stevens
Photographer: Russel Sadur
Picture Research: Giulia Hetherington
Production Manager: Martin Croshaw

Thank you to our models:
Sue Ottman with Marti, Bernie, and Rosie
Jan Beatens with Ozzie
Angie and Gary Billington with Benson
Karen Tapley with Taf

Picture Acknowledgments

Special photography © Octopus Publishing Group Limited/Russel Sadur

Other photography: 4–5 Alamy/Aflo Foto Agency; 7 Getty Images/National Geographic/Jim and Jamie Dutcher; 8 Getty Images; 9 Getty Images/Photographic's Choice/Steve Smith; 13 Getty Images/Gone Wild; 14 Corbis/Martin Harvey; 17, 19, 20 Alamy/Juniors Bildarchiv; 21 Alamy/Terry Whittaker; 23 Corbis/dpa/Gambarini Mauricio; 25 Shutterstock/Piotr Sikora; 27 Corbis/Jim Craigmyle; 28 FLPA/Angela Hammond; 29 FLPA/John Watkins; 30 Corbis/zefa/Staffan Widstrand; 35 Alamy/Daniel Dempster Photography; 37 Alamy/blickwinkel; 38 Ardea.com/John Daniels; 39 iStockphoto/Brent Melton; 41 Naturepl.com/Adriano Bacchella; 42 Getty Images/Barbara Peacock; 45 Getty Images/Tomonori Taniguchi; 46 Getty Images/Neo Vision; 50 Rex Features; 51 Naturepl.com/Wegner/ARCO; 52 Alamy/Kathy Wright; 53 Alamy/Juniors Bildarchiv; 54 Getty Images/Jim Corwin; 55 Alamy/Linn Arvidsson; 57 Alamy/Michael Clark; 58 Shutterstock/Dewayne Flowers; 61 Corbis/Herbert Spichtinger/zefa; 65 Naturepl.com/Jason Smalley; 67 Ardea.com/Rolf Kopfle; 69 Alamy/ImageState/Martin Ruegner; 71 Getty Images/altrendo nature; 73 Ardea.com/Jean Michel Labat; 75 Photolibrary Group/Juniors Bildarchiv; 77 Corbis/Dale C Spartas; 78 Alamy/Arco Images; 79 Photolibrary Group/Juniors Bildarchiv; 80 Corbis/zefa/Herbert Spichtinger; 84 Ardea.com/John Daniels; 99 Getty Images/GK Hart/Vikki Hart; 100 Ardea.com/Jean Michel Labat; 116 Corbis/Jim Craigmyle; 129 Octopus Publishing Group/Russell Sadur; 131 Alamy/Petra Wegner; 135 Shutterstock/Nick Stubbs; 137 Shutterstock/Sarit Saliman; 139 Corbis/Dale C Spartas.